CAMBRIDGE
UNIVERSITY PRESS

Cambridge Lower Secondary
Science

WORKBOOK 9

Mary Jones, Diane Fellowes-Freeman & Michael Smyth

CAMBRIDGE
UNIVERSITY PRESS

University Printing House, Cambridge CB2 8BS, United Kingdom

One Liberty Plaza, 20th Floor, New York, NY 10006, USA

477 Williamstown Road, Port Melbourne, VIC 3207, Australia

314–321, 3rd Floor, Plot 3, Splendor Forum, Jasola District Centre, New Delhi – 110025, India

103 Penang Road, #05–06/07, Visioncrest Commercial, Singapore 238467

Cambridge University Press is part of the University of Cambridge.

It furthers the University's mission by disseminating knowledge in the pursuit of education, learning and research at the highest international levels of excellence.

www.cambridge.org
Information on this title: www.cambridge.org/9781108742894

First published 2013
Second edition 2021

20 19 18 17 16 15 14

Printed in India by Multivista Global Pvt Ltd.

A catalogue record for this publication is available from the British Library

ISBN 978-1-108-74289-4 Paperback with Digital Access (1 year)

The exercises in this Workbook have been written to cover the Biology, Chemistry, Physics, Earth and Space and any appropriate Thinking and Working Scientifically learning objectives from the Cambridge Lower Secondary Science curriculum framework (0893). Some Thinking and Working Scientifically learning objectives and the Science in Context learning objectives have not been covered in this Workbook.

> Contents

1 Photosynthesis and the carbon cycle

2 Properties of materials

3 Forces and energy

4 Maintaining life

5 Reactivity

6 Sound and space

7 Genes and inheritance

8 Rates of reaction

9 Electricity

> How to use this book

This workbook provides questions for you to practise what you have learnt in class. There is a topic to match each topic in your Learner's Book. Each topic contains the following sections:

Focus: these questions help you to master the basics ⟶

Focus

In this exercise, you will decide which variables to keep the same in an experiment. You will put results into a table and make a conclusion.

Arun does an experiment to investigate whether plants photosynthesise faster when they have more light.

The diagram shows the apparatus he uses.

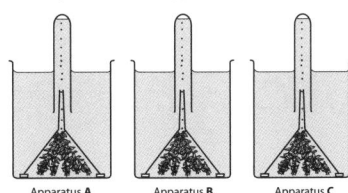

Apparatus **A**   Apparatus **B**   Apparatus **C**

Arun puts Apparatus **A** next to a window.

He puts Apparatus **B** in a shady corner of the same room.

He puts Apparatus **C** in a dark cupboard.

Practice: these questions help you to become more confident in using what you have learnt ⟶

Practice

In this exercise, you will provide explanations using your scientific knowledge.

Zara found a plant that had leaves with some green areas and some white areas. Leaves like this are called variegated leaves.

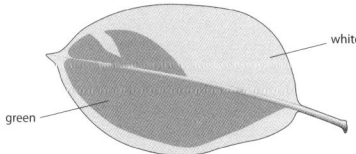

white

green

She decided to test one of the leaves for starch using iodine solution. She made this prediction:

The green parts of the leaf will contain starch, but the white parts will not.

Challenge: these questions will make you think very hard ⟶

Challenge

In this task, you will interpret the results of an experiment. You will think about variables, write a conclusion and use your scientific knowledge to explain a set of results.

Sofia and Zara do an experiment to investigate photosynthesis.

They cut ten little discs out of a leaf. Each disc is exactly the same size and is cut from the same leaf.

They put one disc into water in a small beaker and shine light onto it.

Little bubbles appear on the underside of the leaf disc.

After a while, the bubbles of gas make the leaf disc float to the surface of the water.

Sofia and Zara record the time taken for the leaf disc to float to the surface, then repeat their experiment with four more leaf discs.

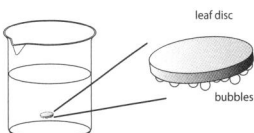

leaf disc

bubbles

1 ▸ Photosynthesis and the carbon cycle

› 1.1 Photosynthesis

Exercise 1.1A How light level affects photosynthesis

Focus

In this exercise, you will decide which variables to keep the same in an experiment. You will put results into a table and make a conclusion.

Arun does an experiment to investigate whether plants photosynthesise faster when they have more light.

The diagram shows the apparatus he uses.

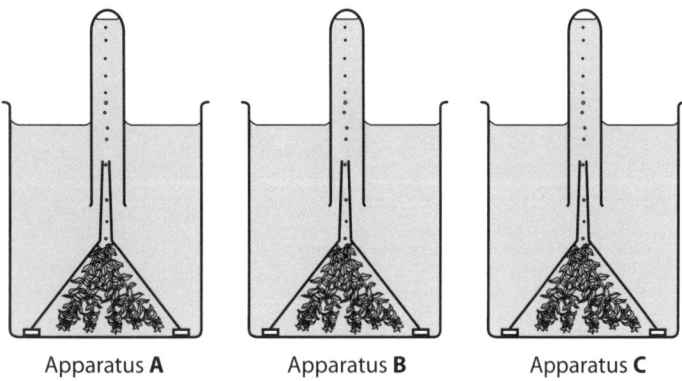

Apparatus **A**   Apparatus **B**   Apparatus **C**

Arun puts Apparatus **A** next to a window.

He puts Apparatus **B** in a shady corner of the same room.

He puts Apparatus **C** in a dark cupboard.

1 What should Arun try to keep the same for all three sets of apparatus?

Tick (✓) **three** boxes.

the amount of light ☐

the type of plant ☐

the mass of the plant ☐

the number of bubbles ☐

the temperature ☐

Arun leaves his three sets of apparatus for two days.
Then he measures the volume of gas collected in each
test tube.

This is what he writes down.

A 18.3 cm³

B 7.2 cm³

C 0.5 cm³

2 Complete Arun's results table.

Apparatus	Amount of light	
A		
B		
C		

3 What conclusion can Arun make from his results?

Tick (✓) **one** box.

Plants need chlorophyll for photosynthesis. ☐

Plants that live in water photosynthesise more slowly
than plants that live on land. ☐

Plants photosynthesise faster when they have more light. ☐

Plants use water for photosynthesis. ☐

Exercise 1.1B The effect of different colours of light on the rate of photosynthesis

Practice

This exercise gives you practice in recording results, and also thinking about variables in an experiment.

Marcus wanted to find out which colour of light would make a plant photosynthesise fastest.

The diagram shows the apparatus that he set up.

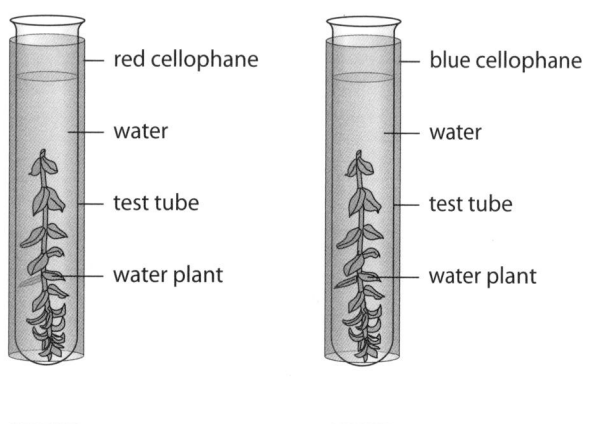

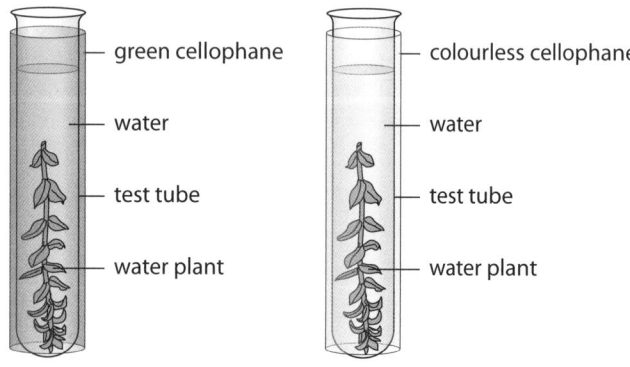

Marcus shone a light onto each tube. He counted the number of bubbles that the water plant gave off in one minute. He did this three times for each water plant.

These are his results.

red – 10, 12, 11   blue – 8, 12, 10

green – 4, 5, 6   colourless – 11, 13, 12

1   What was the variable that Marcus changed in his experiment?

....

2   What was the variable that Marcus measured in his experiment?

....

....

3   List three variables that Marcus should have kept the same in his experiment.

first variable ....

second variable ....

third variable ....

4   Draw a results table in the space below, and fill in Marcus's results so that they are easy to understand. Remember to include a column where you can write in the mean value for each set of results.

5 Complete the bar chart to show Marcus's results.

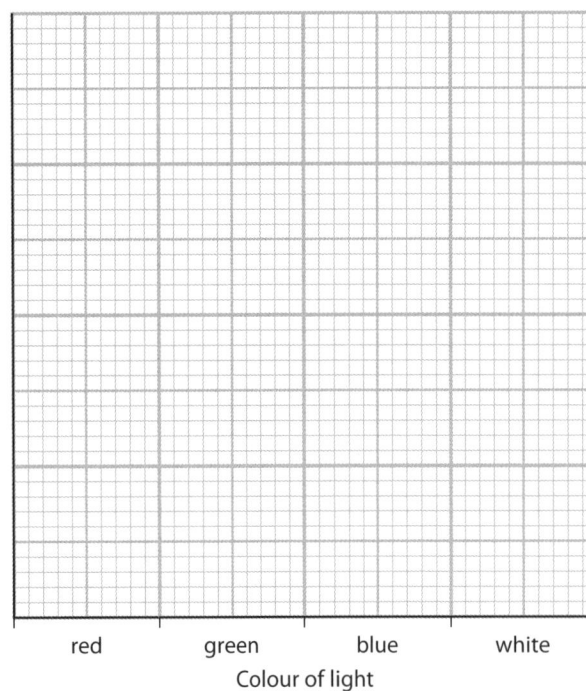

red   green   blue   white
Colour of light

6 Write down a conclusion that Marcus can make from his results.

....

....

....

Exercise 1.1C Turning an idea into a hypothesis that can be tested

Challenge

In this challenging task, you will choose an idea and then turn it into a hypothesis that can be tested by scientific experiment. Then you will write a plan for the experiment.

Here is an idea about water plants and photosynthesis.

Idea: Carbon dioxide is one of the raw materials for photosynthesis. We can provide extra carbon dioxide to a water plant by bubbling carbon dioxide gas into the water. This could allow the water plant to photosynthesise faster.

1   Use the idea to write down a hypothesis that you could test by
    doing an experiment.

    Check your hypothesis with your teacher before you move on to
    question 2.

    ....

    ....

    ....

2   Use this page and the next to write a plan for an experiment you
    could do to test your hypothesis.

    •   Try to make your plan really clear and detailed, so that
        someone else could follow it to do your experiment.

    •   Include a labelled diagram of the apparatus you would use.

    •   Draw a results chart with headings.

    •   Predict what you think the results might be, giving a reason for
        your prediction.

    •   Remember to state your independent variable, dependent
        variable and the variables that you will try to keep the same.

    ....

    ....

    ....

    ....

    ....

    ....

    ....

    ....

    ....

    ....

    ....

....

....

....

....

....

....

....

....

....

....

....

....

....

....

....

....

....

....

....

....

....

> 1.2 More about photosynthesis

Exercise 1.2A Duckweed experiment

Focus

In this exercise, you will practise planning experiments, recording results and making conclusions.

Sofia does an experiment to find out if extra nitrate fertiliser helps duckweed plants to grow and reproduce faster.

She takes five dishes and puts the same volume of distilled water into each of them. She labels the dishes **A**, **B**, **C**, **D** and **E**.

She adds one grain of fertiliser to dish **B**, two grains to dish **C**, three grains to dish **D** and four grains to dish **E**.

She puts five duckweed plants into each dish.

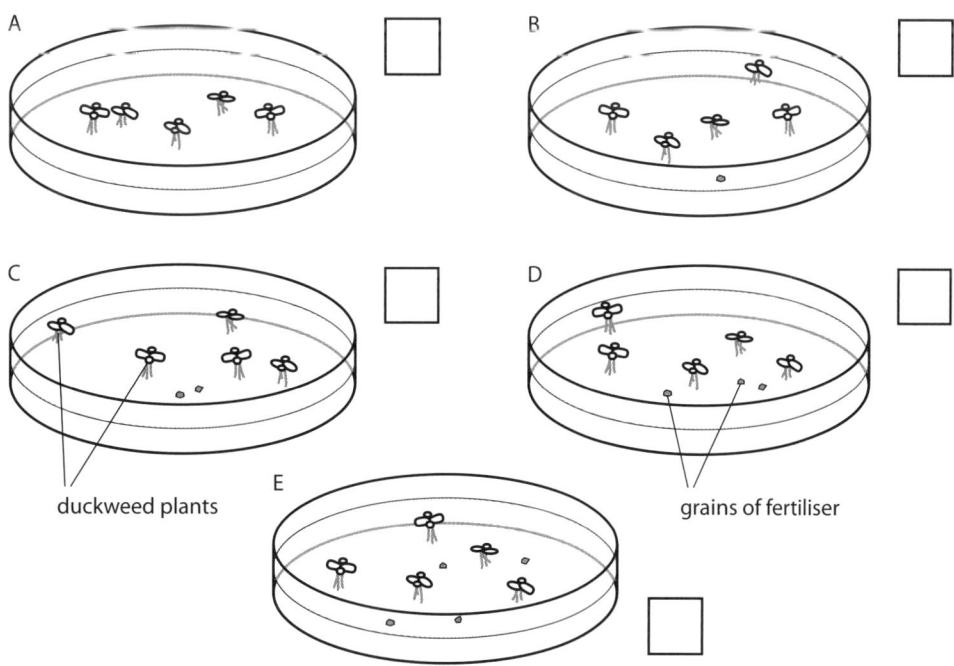

duckweed plants   grains of fertiliser

1 Write the number of grains of fertiliser that Sofia puts into each dish in the boxes next to each diagram.

2 Which variable does Sofia change in her experiment?
Tick (✓) the correct answer.

number of duckweed plants ☐

volume of water ☐

quantity of fertiliser ☐

3 Which variables should Sofia keep the same in her experiment?
Tick (✓) all the correct answers.

number of duckweed plants ☐

quantity of fertiliser ☐

light intensity ☐

volume of water ☐

temperature ☐

After two weeks, Sofia counts the number of duckweed plants in each dish. She writes the results in her notebook.

A 5 plants   B 9 plants

C 10 plants   D 8 plants

E no plants

4 Complete the results chart.

Dish	Number of grains of fertiliser	Number of plants at end of experiment
A	0	5

5 Draw a bar chart to display Sofia's results.

Put 'number of grains of fertiliser' on the horizontal axis.

Put 'number of plants at end of experiment' on the vertical axis.

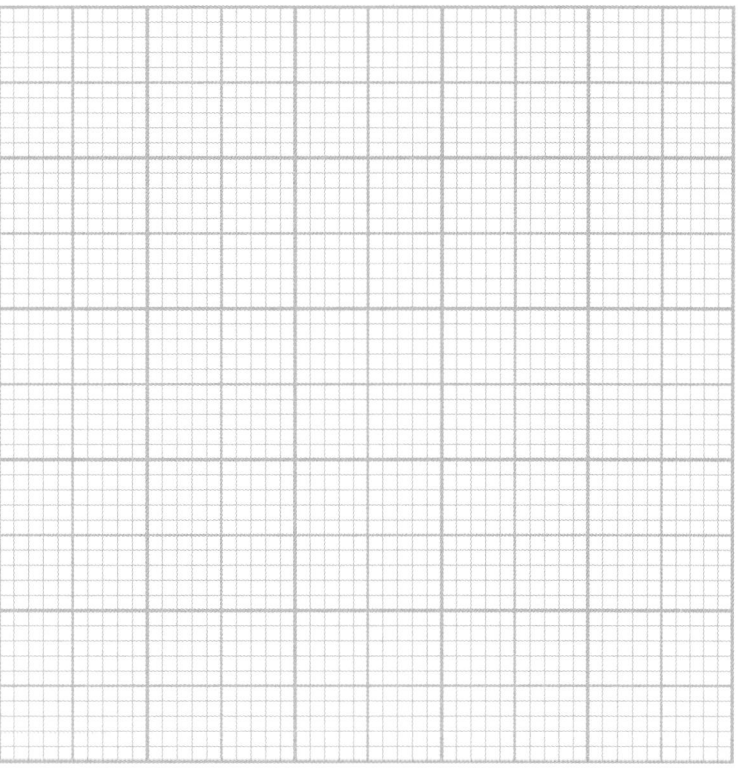

Sofia says:

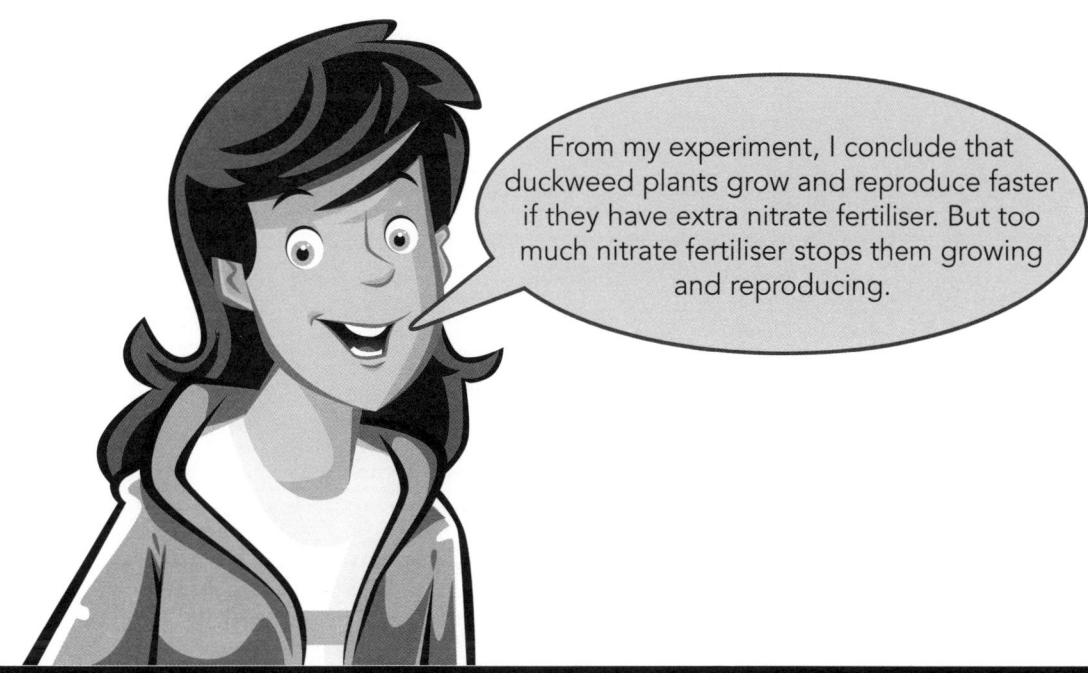

From my experiment, I conclude that duckweed plants grow and reproduce faster if they have extra nitrate fertiliser. But too much nitrate fertiliser stops them growing and reproducing.

6 Explain how Sofia's results support her conclusion.

....

....

....

....

....

7 How can Sofia improve her experiment?

Tick (✓) the correct answer.

Use three sets of dishes for each quantity of fertiliser. ☐

Use a different kind of water plant in each dish. ☐

Put each dish in a different temperature. ☐

Exercise 1.2B Testing a variegated leaf for starch

Practice

In this exercise, you will provide explanations using your scientific knowledge.

Zara found a plant that had leaves with some green areas and some white areas. Leaves like this are called variegated leaves.

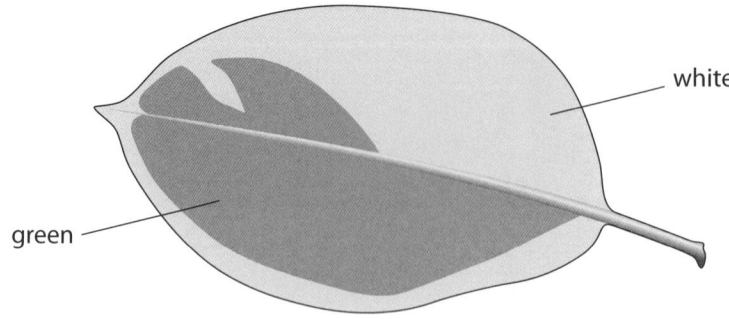

She decided to test one of the leaves for starch using iodine solution. She made this prediction:

The green parts of the leaf will contain starch, but the white parts will not.

1   What is the substance that makes leaves green?

    ....

2   Explain why Zara's prediction is likely to be correct.

    ....

    ....

3   First, Zara put the leaf into boiling water, and left it there for
    5 minutes.

    Explain why she did this.

    ....

    ....

4   Next, she took the leaf out of the water and put it into some
    hot alcohol.

    Explain why she did this.

    ....

    ....

5   Lastly, Zara dipped the leaf into water and spread it out on a white
    tile. The leaf looked white.

    She added iodine solution to the leaf. Some parts of the leaf went
    orange-brown, and some went blue-black.

    On the diagram below, shade in the parts of the leaf that would go
    blue-black, if Zara's prediction was correct.

6   What substance causes the iodine to turn blue-black?

    ....

Exercise 1.2C Floating discs experiment

Challenge

In this task, you will interpret the results of an experiment. You will think about variables, write a conclusion and use your scientific knowledge to explain a set of results.

Sofia and Zara do an experiment to investigate photosynthesis.

They cut ten little discs out of a leaf. Each disc is exactly the same size and is cut from the same leaf.

They put one disc into water in a small beaker and shine light onto it.

Little bubbles appear on the underside of the leaf disc.

After a while, the bubbles of gas make the leaf disc float to the surface of the water.

Sofia and Zara record the time taken for the leaf disc to float to the surface, then repeat their experiment with four more leaf discs.

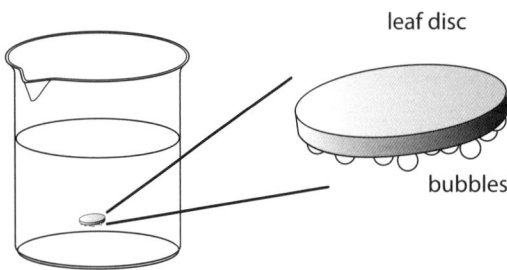

leaf disc

bubbles

1 Name the gas that the leaf disc produced when it photosynthesised.

....

2 Explain why the bubbles of gas formed on the underside of the leaf, not on the top.

....

....

3 In what way does the time taken for the leaf disc to rise and float depend on the bubbles of gas? Explain your answer.

....

....

....

Sofia and Zara do the investigation again, but this time they put the beaker and the leaf discs in a room with only dim lighting.

Here are the girls' results from both tests.

Conditions	Time taken for leaf disc to rise to the surface, in seconds					
	Try 1	Try 2	Try 3	Try 4	Try 5	Mean
bright light	14	3	12	14	11	
dim light	44	66	69	77	71	

4   Suggest the hypothesis that the girls were testing.

    ....

    ....

5   What was the independent variable in the girls' experiment?

    ....

    ....

6   Sofia thought that there was one anomalous result in each row of their results table.

    Draw circles around the two anomalous results in the table.

7   Calculate the mean time taken for each row in the results table. Write your answers in the last column.

    Remember not to include anomalous results when you calculate the mean.

8   Suggest why the times taken for the five leaf discs to rise in each of

the lighting conditions were not all the same.

....

....

....

....

9   Write a conclusion for the girls' experiment.

....

....

10   Suggest an explanation for the difference between the mean times for the leaf discs to rise in bright light and in dim light.

....

....

....

> 1.3 The carbon cycle

Exercise 1.3 Completing a carbon cycle diagram

The diagram shows part of the carbon cycle.

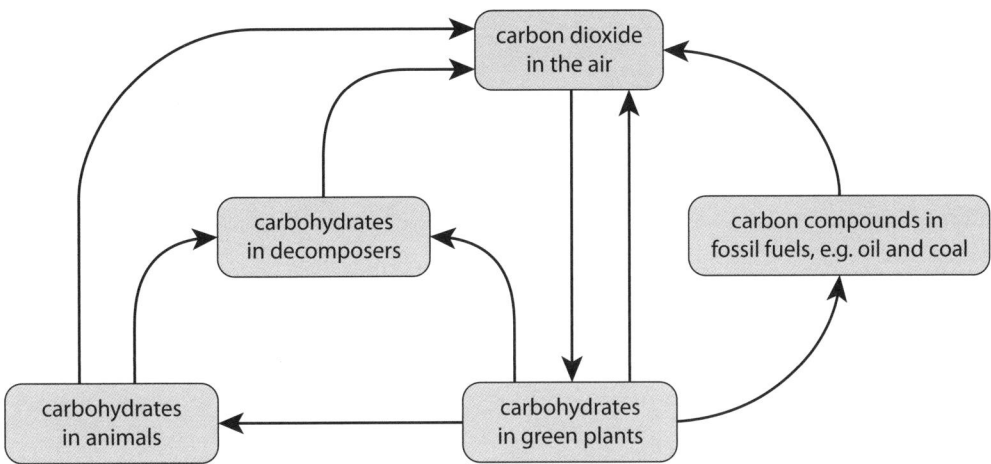

Focus

1   On the diagram, write these labels next to the correct arrows:

   R next to the three arrows that show respiration

   P next to the one arrow that shows photosynthesis

   C next to the one arrow that shows fossil fuels being formed

   D next to the two arrows that show decomposition

   F next to the one arrow that shows feeding.

Practice

Hydrogencarbonate indicator changes colour according to how much carbon dioxide there is in it.

*   The indicator is purple when there is no carbon dioxide.

*   The indicator is red when there is a low concentration of carbon dioxide.

*   The indicator is yellow when there is a high concentration of carbon dioxide.

Arun set up four boiling tubes like this:

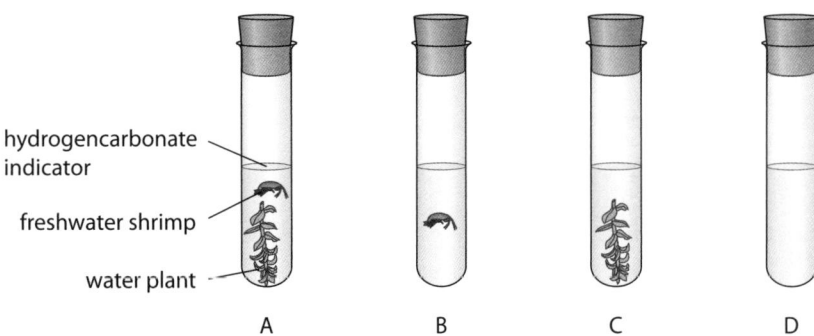

hydrogencarbonate
indicator

freshwater shrimp

water plant

A   B   C   D

Arun recorded the colour of the indicator in each tube at the start of his experiment. Then he left the tubes in the laboratory for two hours, and recorded the colour again.

This is what he wrote down.

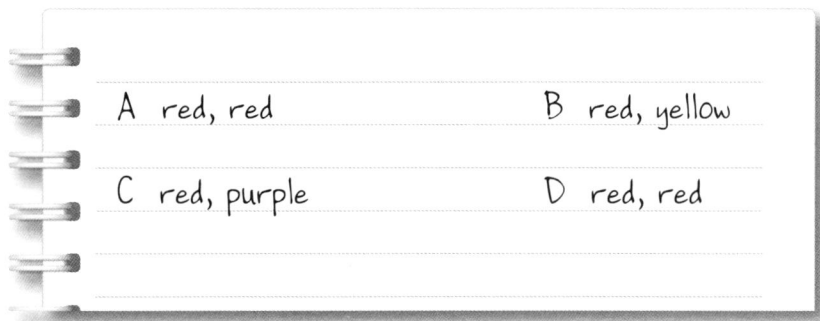

A red, red   B red, yellow

C red, purple   D red, red

2   Suggest why Arun put a bung in each tube.

....

....

3   Name two variables that Arun kept the same in his experiment.

....

....

4 Construct a results table in the space below, and complete it to show Arun's results.

5 Explain Arun's results.

....

....

....

....

....

....

....

Challenge

6 Use Arun's results, and the diagram of the carbon cycle, to explain the importance of plants in maintaining a stable concentration of carbon dioxide in the atmosphere.

....

....

....

....

....

....

> 1.4 Climate change

Exercise 1.4 Interpreting graphs about climate change

In this exercise, you will look at graphs displaying data collected by NASA (the USA's National Aeronatutics and Space Adminstration) and NOAA (the USA's National Oceanic and Atmosphere Adminstration). You will need to study the graphs carefully to answer the questions, and also use your own knowledge about photosynthesis, the carbon cycle and climate change.

Focus

Here are three graphs about climate change.

Graph A

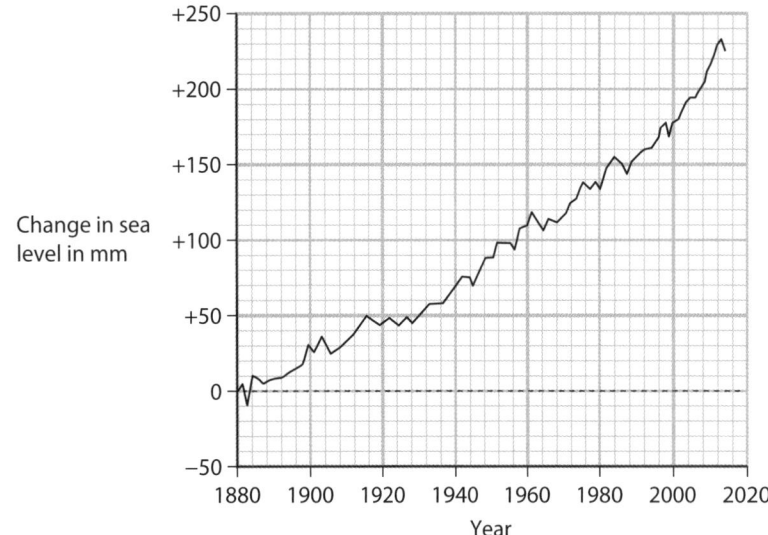

Graph B

Extent of sea ice in the Bering Sea (in the Arctic) in millions of km²

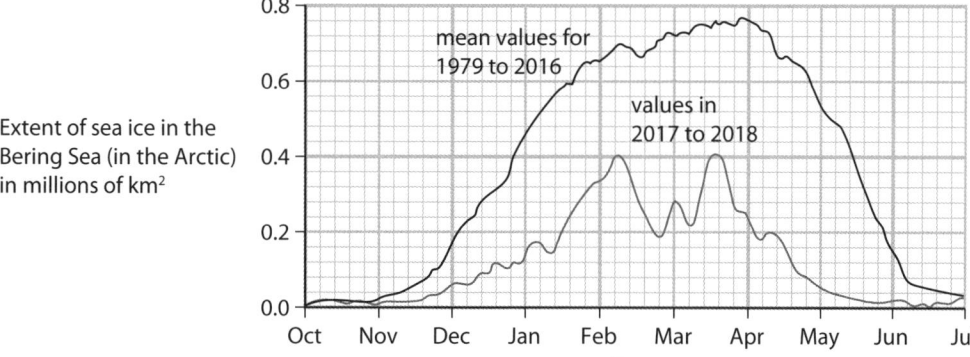

Graph C

Percentage carbon dioxide concentration in the atmosphere

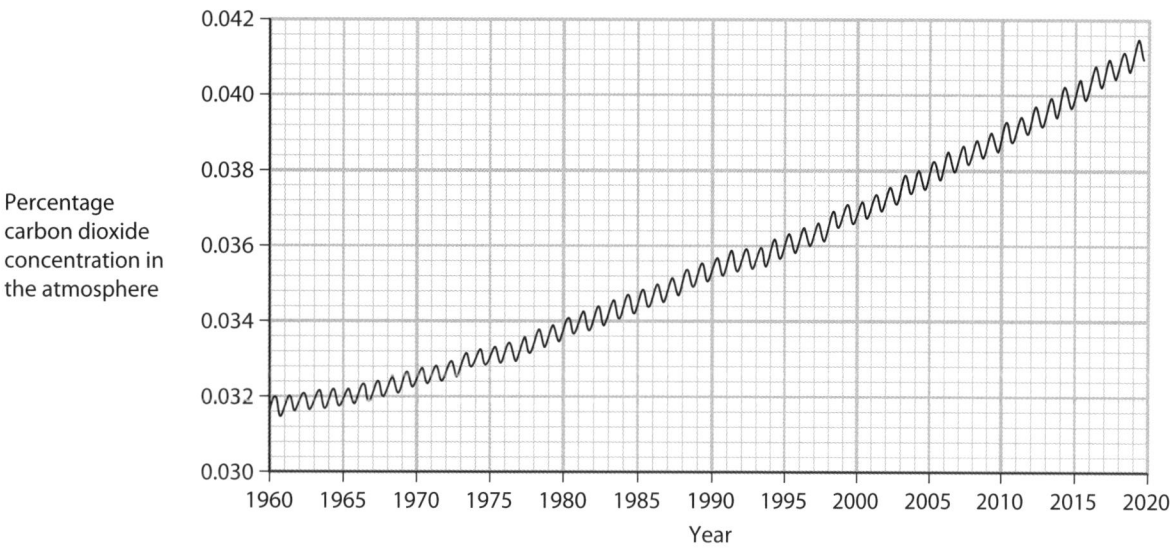

1   Write the **letter** of the graph that matches each of these statements.

There is more carbon dioxide in the atmosphere now than there

used to be. ....

Sea level is steadily rising. ....

Sea ice in the Arctic is present for fewer months in the year now,

and there is less of it. ....

Practice

2 Look at graph **A**.

Describe in words what is shown on the graph. Include some figures in your answer, for example by stating the change in sea level since 1880.

....

....

....

....

....

3 Look at graph **B**.

Describe **two** ways in which the extent of sea ice in the Bering Sea in 2017 to 2018 differed from the mean extent from 1979 to 2016.

1st way ....

....

2nd way ....

....

Challenge

4 Look at graph B again.

What extra data would you want to collect, in order to be certain that the extent of sea ice really is changing? Explain your answer.

....

....

....

....

5   Look at graph **C**.

Most scientists think that human activities are contributing to the changes in carbon dioxide concentration shown in the graph.

Use your own knowledge to explain why they think this.

....

....

....

....

....

6   Look at graph **C** again.

The measurements of carbon dioxide concentration were made in Hawaii, which is in the northern hemisphere.

Thinking about plants and photosynthesis, suggest why the line wiggles up and down (varies throughout) each year.

....

....

....

....

....

2 ▶ Properties of materials

> 2.1 Atomic structure and the Periodic Table

Exercise 2.1 Atomic structure

All parts of this exercise will help you to use the Periodic Table to find information about the structure of the atoms of elements.

You will need to use the information in the Periodic Table to answer the following questions.

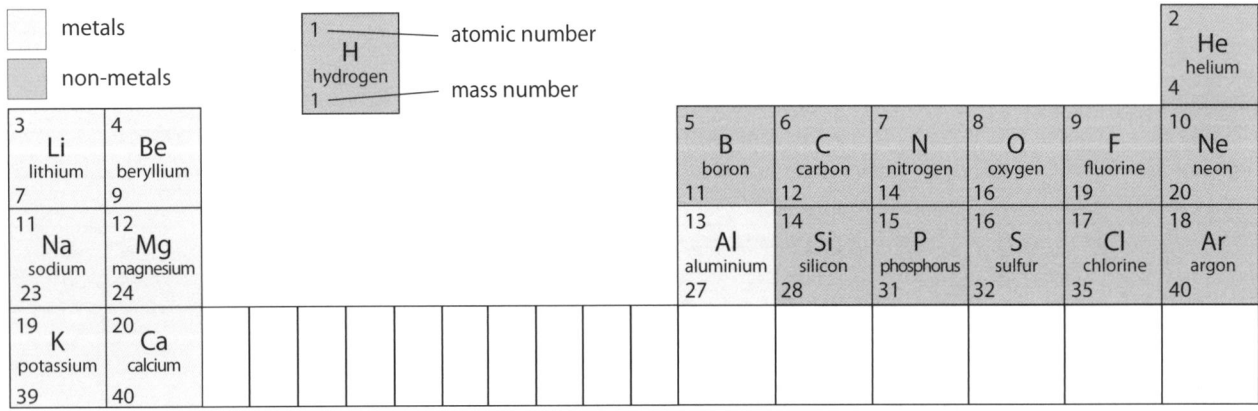

Focus

The atoms of one element are different from the atoms of all other elements. They have different atomic numbers and mass numbers.

The smaller of the two numbers in each square is the atomic number and the larger of the two numbers is the mass number.

1   What is the atomic number for magnesium? ....

2   What is the mass number for nitrogen? ....

3   Which element has the atomic number 13? ....

4   Which element has the mass number 20? ....

Atoms of different elements have different numbers of protons, neutrons and electrons.

Look at this example:

Lithium

Atomic number = 3

Mass number = 7

Number of protons = 3

Number of neutrons = 7 − 3 = 4

Number of electrons = 3 (always the same as the number of protons)

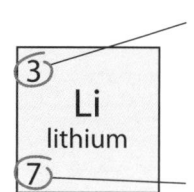

The atomic number tells you how many protons there are.

The mass number tells you how many protons plus neutrons there are.

5   Complete these numbers for a boron atom.

   Boron

   Atomic number = ...

   Mass number = ...

   Number of protons = ...

   Number of neutrons = ...

   Number of electrons = ...

Practice

6 The element carbon has an atomic number of 6 and a mass number of 12.

   a How many protons does a carbon atom have? ....

   b How many electrons does a carbon atom have? ....

   c How many neutrons does a carbon atom have? ....

   d Draw and label the structure of an atom of carbon.

7 Complete the table.

Element	Atomic number	Mass number	Protons	Neutrons	Electrons	Electronic structure
beryllium	4	9	4	5	4	2,2
phosphorus	15	31				
calcium	20	40				

Challenge

8 As you move along a row in the Periodic Table from left to right, and then along to the next row from left to right, the atomic number and the mass number change.

Look carefully. Describe these changes.

The atomic number ....

....

....

The mass number ....

....

....

9 Which two elements have the same mass number?

....

10 Name an element that is a gas and has the same number of neutrons as protons.

....

11 Complete the table and identify the element.

Element:	
atomic number	
mass number	
number of protons	19
number of neutrons	20
number of electrons	
electronic structure	

> 2.2 Trends in groups within the Periodic Table

Exercise 2.2A Elements in the same group

Focus

In this exercise you compare the structure of atoms in Group 1.

Elements in the same group are similar.

Lithium, sodium and potassium are elements in Group 1.

They are all metals.

1   What can you say about the number of protons in these three metals as you look down the group?

....

2   What can you say about the mass number of these three metals as you look down the group?

....

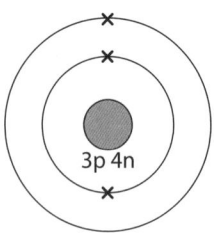

lithium

- Lithium has electrons arranged in two shells.
- It has two electrons in the first (inner) shell, and one in the second, outer shell.
- This is shown as 2,1.
  It is called the electronic structure.

3   This diagram shows the structure of the sodium atom.
     Complete these numbers for sodium:

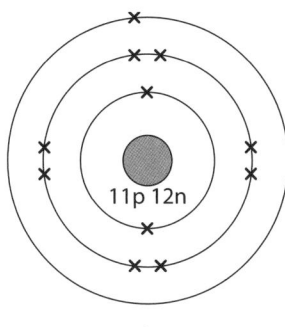

sodium

Atomic number = ...

Mass number = ...

Number of protons = ...

Number of neutrons = ...

Number of electrons = ...

4   Write the electronic structure of sodium. ....

5   What is similar about the structures of an atom of lithium and an
     atom of sodium?

     ....

     ....

6   This diagram shows the structure of the potassium atom.
     Complete these numbers for potassium:

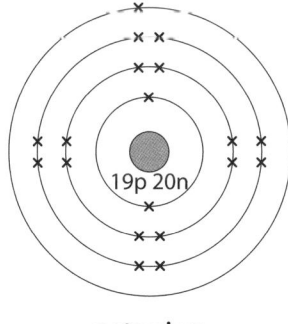

potassium

Atomic number = ...

Mass number = ...

Number of protons = ...

Number of neutrons = ...

Number of electrons = ...

7   Write the electronic structure of potassium ....

8   Compare the structure of the atoms of these three metals in Group 1.
     What is similar about their structure?

     ....

     ....

     ....

9 What is different about the three atoms? Try to state two differences.

....

....

....

....

Exercise 2.2B Trends in groups within the Periodic Table

Practice

This exercise will help you to identify trends in groups of the Periodic Table.

1 Explain what is meant by a 'group' in the Periodic Table.

....

2 This table contains some data about the elements in Group 7 of the Periodic Table. The elements are given in descending order.

Element	Atomic number	Mass number	Melting point in °C	Boiling point in °C	Reactivity
fluorine	9	19	−220	−188	most reactive
chlorine	17	35	−101	−34	
bromine	35	80	−7	59	less reactive
iodine	53				
astatine	85				

a What trends can you see in this group of the Periodic Table?

....

....

....

b Iodine is the fourth element in this group. Would you expect the melting point of iodine to be higher or lower than that of bromine?

....

c Would you expect iodine to be a solid, a liquid or a gas at room temperature? Give a reason for your answer.

....

d Would you expect iodine to have a higher or lower boiling point than astatine? Give a reason for your answer.

....

e Would you expect astatine to be more or less reactive than iodine?

....

Exercise 2.2C Comparing trends in Groups 1 and 7

Challenge

In this challenge exercise, you will use information to compare elements in the same group.

Group 1

Element	Atomic number	Mass number	Melting point in °C	Boiling point in °C
lithium	3	7	180	1360
sodium	11	23	98	900
potassium	19	39	63	777

Group 7

Element	Atomic number	Mass number	Melting point in °C	Boiling point in °C
fluorine	9	19	−220	−188
chlorine	17	35	−101	−34
bromine	35	80	−7	59

Use the information to answer the questions.

1   As the atomic numbers in Group 1 increase, what happens to the melting point?

....

2   As the atomic numbers in Group 7 increase, what happens to the melting point?

....

....

3   Compare the trends in boiling points in Group 1 and Group 7.

....

....

In Group 1 the least reactive shown in the table is lithium; the most reactive is potassium.

In Group 7 the least reactive shown in the table is bromine; the most reactive is fluorine.

4   Describe how reactivity relates to the size of the atoms in each group.

In Group 1:

....

....

In Group 7:

....

....

5   The elements that come next in each group, in order of atomic number, are:

- rubidium in Group 1

- iodine in Group 7.

Make predictions about the reactivity, melting point and boiling point of rubidium and iodine, compared with the other elements in their group.

Rubidium, Group 1

Reactivity: ....

Melting point: ....

Boiling point: ....

Iodine, Group 7

Reactivity: ....

Melting point: ....

Boiling point: ....

> 2.3 Why elements react to form compounds

Exercise 2.3A Atoms and ions

Focus

This exercise will help you to show the difference between an atom and an ion.

1   This diagram shows the structure of a lithium atom.
     Label the electron shell with the highest energy level.

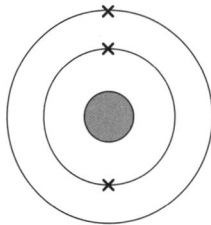

2   Draw a diagram to show the structure of a lithium ion.

3   The symbol for a lithium atom is Li.
     What is the symbol for a lithium ion?

     ....

4   This diagram shows the structure of a fluorine atom.

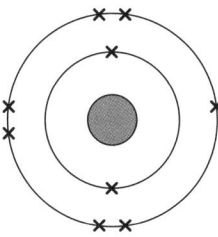

Draw a diagram to show the structure of a fluorine ion.

5   The symbol for a fluorine atom is F.
     What is the symbol for a fluorine ion?

     ....

Exercise 2.3B Why do ions form?

Practice

In this exercise, you will practise drawing atoms and ions and explain why ions form.

1   Using the information here, draw atoms and ions of sodium and chlorine in the spaces below.

sodium	chlorine
atomic number 11	atomic number 17
mass number 23	mass number 35
sodium atom:	chlorine atom:
sodium ion:	chlorine ion:

2   How are the electrons in an atom held in place?

....

3   Why are ions formed?

....

....

Exercise 2.3C Forming ionic compounds (extension material)

Challenge

In this exercise, you will draw diagrams to illustrate the formation of ionic compounds.

1   When calcium reacts with chlorine the compound calcium chloride is formed. The formula for calcium chloride is $CaCl_2$.

> Information you may need:
>
> Calcium has an atomic number of 20 and a mass number of 40.
>
> Chlorine has an atomic number of 17 and a mass number of 35.

    a   Draw diagrams to show the structures of calcium and chlorine atoms. Make sure you label the calcium and chlorine atoms.

    b   Draw diagrams to show the ions of calcium and chlorine. Make sure you label the calcium and chlorine ions.

c Explain why the formula for calcium chloride is $CaCl_2$.
You may use diagrams to help you explain.

....

....

....

....

....

....

....

....

> 2.4 Simple and giant structures

Exercise 2.4A Ionic or covalent bonds

Focus

This exercise will help you to distinguish between ionic and covalent substances.

Look at the diagrams that show the structures of two substances A and B.

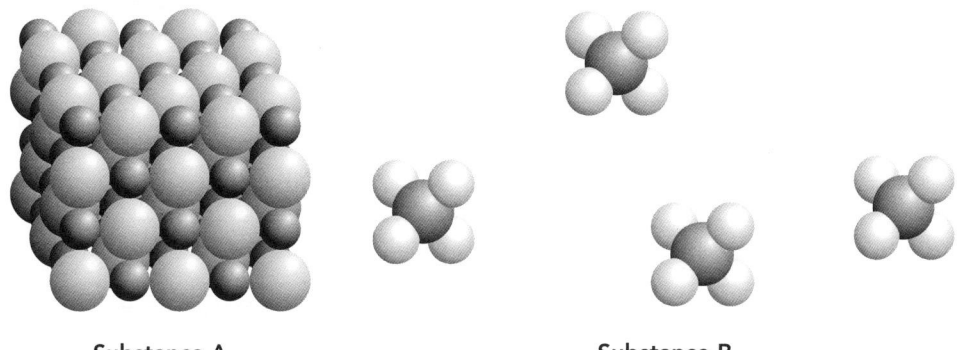

Substance A   Substance B

1   What type of bonding do you think substance A has?
    Give a reason for your answer.

    ....

2   On the illustration above, label substance B to show where there are strong forces.

3   Which substance has bonds where electrons are shared?

    ....

4   Which substance has a lattice structure? ....

5   A substance when dissolved in water conducts electricity.
    What type of bonding does it have?

    ....

6   Some giant structures such as diamond are called macromolecules.
    What type of bonding is found in a diamond macromolecule?

    ....

7   Give an example of a macromolecule other than diamond.

    ....

Exercise 2.4B Properties of ionic and covalent substances

Practice

In this exercise, you will identify properties of substances linked to their structures.

Look carefully at the table and answer the questions.

Substance	Melting point in °C	Boiling point in °C	Solid, liquid or gas at room temperature?	Ionic or simple molecule with covalent bonds
potassium chloride	770	1500		
substance X	−182	−161		
calcium chloride			solid	ionic
ammonia	−77	−34		
magnesium oxide	2825	3600		
bromine	−7	59		
substance Y	0	100	liquid	simple molecule with covalent bonds

1   Calcium chloride is an ionic compound that is solid at room temperature. What does that tell you about its melting and boiling points?

   ....

2   Is substance X a solid, liquid or gas at room temperature?

   ....

3   List the substances that are solids at room temperature.

   ....

4 List the substances, other than substance Y, that have simple molecules with covalent bonds.

....

5 Suggest what substance Y is. Give a reason for your suggestion.

....

6 Which substance, other than substance Y, is a liquid at room temperature?

....

7 Explain why magnesium oxide has high melting and boiling points.

....

....

....

8 Explain why ammonia has low melting and boiling points.

....

....

....

Exercise 2.4C Giant structures of carbon

Challenge

In this exercise you will link the structure of diamond and graphite to their properties.

Diamond and graphite are both giant structures formed from the element carbon.

1   Which of the diagrams below represents the structure of diamond and which represents the structure of graphite?

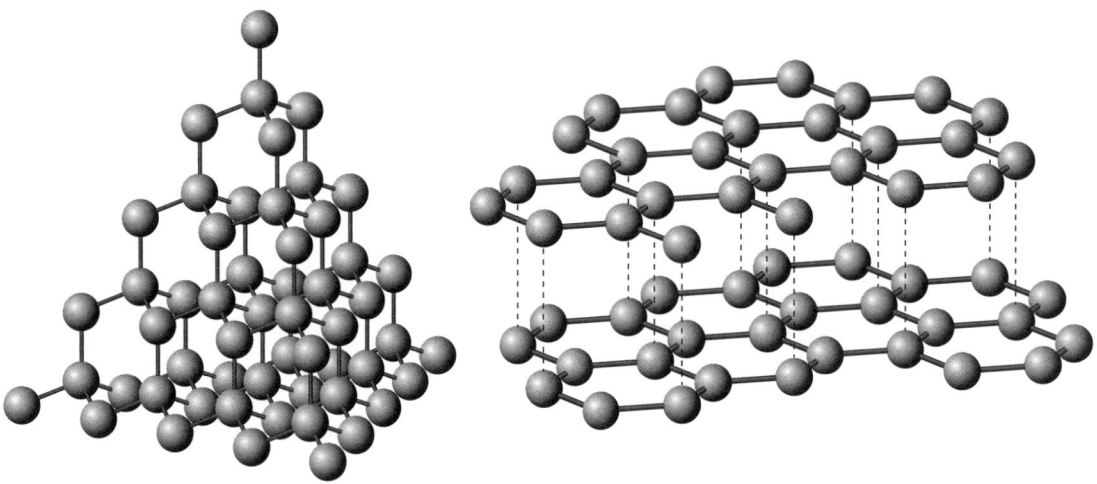

This structure represents: **This structure represents:**

....

2   Graphite is a very soft material.
Explain how its structure is related to its properties.

....

....

....

....

....

3 Diamond is the hardest material on Earth.
Explain how its structure is related to its properties.

....

....

....

....

....

3 ▶ Forces and energy

> 3.1 Density

Exercise 3.1A Comparing densities

Focus

In this exercise, you will compare the densities of different substances.

1   Which of these has the lowest density?

Tick (✓) **one** box.

solid   ☐

liquid   ☐

gas   ☐

2   Marcus has four blocks, A–D, each made from a different type of wood.

All four blocks have the same volume.

The masses of the blocks are:

A   50 g

B   76 g

C   32 g

D   68 g

Which block has the greatest density? Write the letter: ....

3   Zara has four pieces of metal, P–S, each made from a different type of metal.

All four pieces have the same mass.

The volumes of the pieces are:

P   22 cm³   Q   35 cm³   R   19 cm³   S   27 cm³

Which piece of metal has the greatest density?

Write the letter: ....

4   Arun has some solid blocks with different densities.

State how the density of a solid block should compare with water if the block is to float on water.

....

Exercise 3.1B Understanding and calculating density

Practice

In this exercise, you will describe density and calculate some densities.

1   Which of these statements describes density?
     Tick (✓) **one** statement.

     the weight of a substance   ☐

     the volume that a substance occupies   ☐

     the mass of a certain volume of substance   ☐

     the volume of a certain mass of substance   ☐

2   Complete the equation for density.

$$\text{density} = \frac{.....................}{.....................}$$

3   Calculate the density of each of these substances.

    a   A 10 g mass of water that has a volume of 10 cm³.

.... g/cm³

    b   A 170 g mass of brass that has a volume of 20 cm³.

.... g/cm³

    c   A 56 g mass of propane that has a volume of 100 cm³.

.... g/cm³

4   A solid cube is made from copper.
     The lengths of the sides of the cube are 2.0 cm.

    a   Calculate the volume of the cube.

.... cm³

    b   The mass of the cube is 71.2 g.
     Calculate the density of the copper.

.... g/cm³

Exercise 3.1C Density, floating and sinking

Challenge

In this exercise, you will use density to work out whether substances will float or sink.

1   The table shows the densities of four different types of plastic. The plastics are all solids.

type of plastic	density in g/cm³
polyethylene	0.91
polypropylene	0.94
cellulose acetate	1.28
polyvinyl chloride	1.38

The densities of two liquids are:

*   water $1.0 \, \text{g/cm}^3$
*   engine oil $0.92 \, \text{g/cm}^3$

Name **one** type of plastic from the table that will

a   float in both engine oil and in water

    ....

b   sink in engine oil but float in water

    ....

c   sink in both engine oil and in water.

    ....

2 Marcus has a model boat with a volume of 250 cm³.

Calculate the maximum mass of this boat that will float in water.

The density of water is 1.0 g/cm³.

.... g

3 A ship is built using a material called mild steel.
Mild steel has a density of 7.9 g/cm³.

Seawater has a density of 1.03 g/cm³.

Explain how a ship can be made from mild steel and safely float in seawater.

....

....

....

....

....

....

....

> 3.2 Heat and temperature

Exercise 3.2A Heat or temperature

Focus

In this exercise, you will decide whether examples describe heat or temperature.

1 Complete each of the sentences using the word **heat** or **temperature**.

a 100 °C is the .... at which water boils.

b 25 000 J is the quantity of .... needed to make cold water warmer.

c 22 °C is often described as room ....

2 Sofia has two cups of coffee.
The volume of coffee in the cups is the same.

One cup of coffee is at 55 °C.

The other cup of coffee is at 30 °C.

Which statements are true?

Tick (✓) **two** boxes.

The temperature of the coffee in each cup is different. ☐

The temperature of the coffee in each cup is the same. ☐

The heat in the coffee in each cup is different. ☐

The heat in the coffee in each cup is the same. ☐

3 Zara serves two bowls of soup.

In one bowl Zara puts 100 cm³ of soup at 60 °C.

In the other bowl Zara puts 200 cm³ of soup at 60 °C.

Which statements are true?

Tick (✓) **two** boxes.

The temperature of the soup in each bowl is different. ☐

The temperature of the soup in each bowl is the same. ☐

The heat in the soup in each bowl is different. ☐

The heat in the soup in each bowl is the same. ☐

Exercise 3.2B Comparing heat and temperature

Practice

In this exercise, you will describe the difference between heat and temperature.

1   **a**   Write down the unit of temperature. ....

  b   Write down the unit of heat. ....

2   Draw **two** straight lines to match the quantity with the correct description.

Quantity

Description

| the total energy of particles in a substance |

heat

| the maximum energy of particles in a substance |

temperature

| the minimum energy of particles in a substance |

| the average energy of particles in a substance |

3   Complete the sentences using the best words.

In a solid, the particles vibrate about .... positions.

When a solid is heated, the particles vibrate ....

When the temperature of a solid decreases, the particles vibrate

....

4   Two solid blocks of the same material are at 20 °C. One block has double the mass of the other block.

Explain how the heat and temperature of the blocks compare. Use ideas about particles.

heat ....

....

....

temperature ....

....

....

Exercise 3.2C Measuring heat and temperature

Challenge

In this exercise, you will think about measuring heat and temperature.

1 Look at the list of equipment.

   ruler   thermometer   protractor   joule meter   voltmeter

   a Name the equipment from the list that can be used to measure the temperature of water when it is being heated.

   ....

   b Name the equipment from the list that can be used to measure the quantity of heat added to water when it is being heated.

   ....

2 Marcus uses an electric immersion heater to heat water.

   Marcus measures the heat supplied to the water and the temperature of the water at regular intervals. His results are in the table.

quantity of heat supplied in J	temperature of water in °C
0	10
1000	12
2000	14
3000	15
4000	18
5000	20

   a Marcus thinks that one of his results is anomalous.

      i   State which result is anomalous. ....

      ii Describe what Marcus could do about this result.

      ....

      ....

> **b** Use the results in the table to estimate

>> **i** the quantity of heat supplied when the temperature of the water was 19 °C

....

>> **ii** the quantity of heat needed to raise the temperature of the water to 30 °C.

....

〉 3.3 Conservation of energy

Exercise 3.3A What does conservation of energy mean?

Focus

In this exercise, you will think about the meaning of the statement 'conservation of energy'.

1 Which of these will happen when energy is conserved?

Tick (✓) **one** box.

The quantity of energy will increase. ☐

The quantity of energy will stay the same. ☐

A quantity of energy can be made. ☐

A quantity of energy can be destroyed. ☐

2 Which of these shows conservation of energy in an electric lamp?
Tick (✓) **one** box.

Energy input to the lamp equals energy output from the lamp. ☐

Energy input to the lamp is greater than energy output from the lamp. ☐

Energy input to the lamp is less than energy output from the lamp. ☐

The lamp should be switched off when not being used. ☐

3   100 J of electrical energy is supplied to a motor.

The electrical energy is changed to thermal and kinetic energy
in the motor.

Write down the total quantity of thermal and kinetic energy
changed in the motor.

......................................J

4   A car engine changes chemical energy to thermal and kinetic energy.

A total of 3500 J of thermal and kinetic energy are changed.

Write down the quantity of chemical energy changed in the engine.

......................................J

Exercise 3.3B The law of conservation of energy

Practice

In this exercise, you will apply the law of conservation of energy.

1   Write down the law of conservation of energy.

....

....

2   An electric lamp changes electrical energy to light and thermal energy.

Explain how the law of conservation of energy applies to this
electric lamp.

....

....

....

....

3 Sofia takes in more chemical energy from food on days when she is playing sports than on days when she is resting.

Use the law of conservation of energy to explain why.

....

....

....

....

4 An electric motor changes electrical energy into kinetic and thermal energy.

65% of the electrical energy is changed to kinetic energy.

Calculate the percentage of electrical energy changed to thermal energy.

.... %

Exercise 3.3C Calculating energy changes

Challenge

In this exercise, you will use the law of conservation of energy to calculate quantities of energy.

1 An electric lamp takes in 1000 J of electrical energy. The lamp wastes 850 J of energy. Calculate the quantity of useful energy changed by the lamp.

....J

2 A motorcycle engine uses 2400 J of chemical energy in fuel.

The thermal energy changed is 1000 J.

The sound energy changed is 600 J.

The remaining energy is changed to kinetic for movement.

Calculate the quantity of kinetic energy changed by the engine.

....J

3   A television changes electrical energy into thermal, light and sound energy.

50% of the energy is changed to thermal.

30% of the energy is changed to light.

a   Calculate the percentage of the energy changed to sound.

....J

b   (Extension question) Draw a labelled energy flow diagram for the television in the space below.

> 3.4 Moving from hot to cold

Exercise 3.4A Direction of thermal energy transfer 1

Focus

In this exercise, you will think about the direction of the transfer of thermal energy.

1 Complete the sentence using the best word.

Thermal energy is transferred from a place of higher temperature

to a place of .... temperature.

2 Draw an arrow on each of these diagrams to show the direction of thermal energy transfer.

a

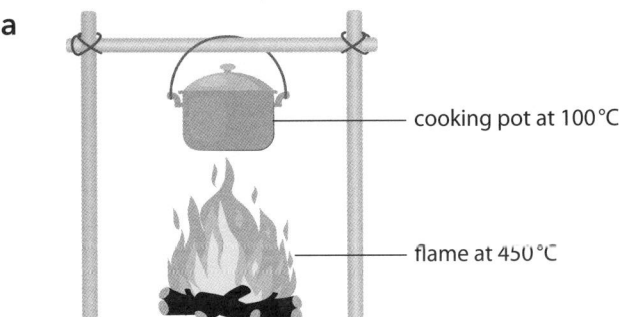

cooking pot at 100 °C

flame at 450 °C

b

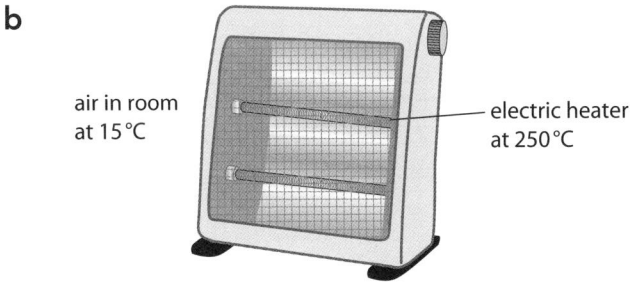

air in room at 15 °C

electric heater at 250 °C

c

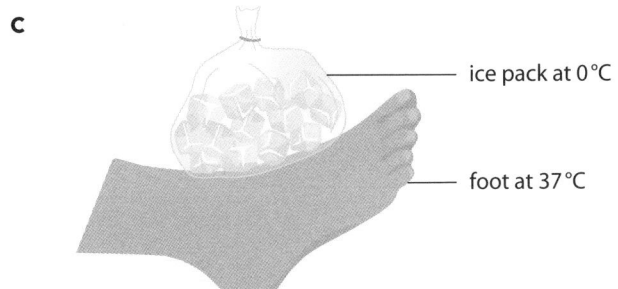

ice pack at 0 °C

foot at 37 °C

Exercise 3.4B Direction of thermal energy transfer 2

Practice

In this exercise, you will think in more detail about thermal energy transfer.

1 Two objects are in contact. The two objects are at different temperatures.

Describe the direction of thermal energy transfer between these two objects.

....

....

....

2 The diagram shows three blocks of metal that are in contact with each other.

The starting temperature of each block is shown.

Draw arrows on the diagram to show the direction of thermal energy transfer between the blocks.

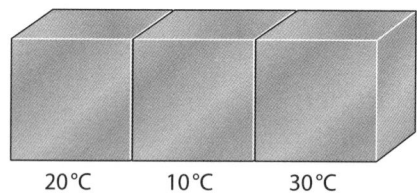

20 °C   10 °C   30 °C

3 A cup of hot tea is at a temperature of 60 °C. The tea is left in a room that is at 25 °C.

Sketch a graph of how the temperature of the tea will change with time. Continue your graph until the temperature of the tea is constant.

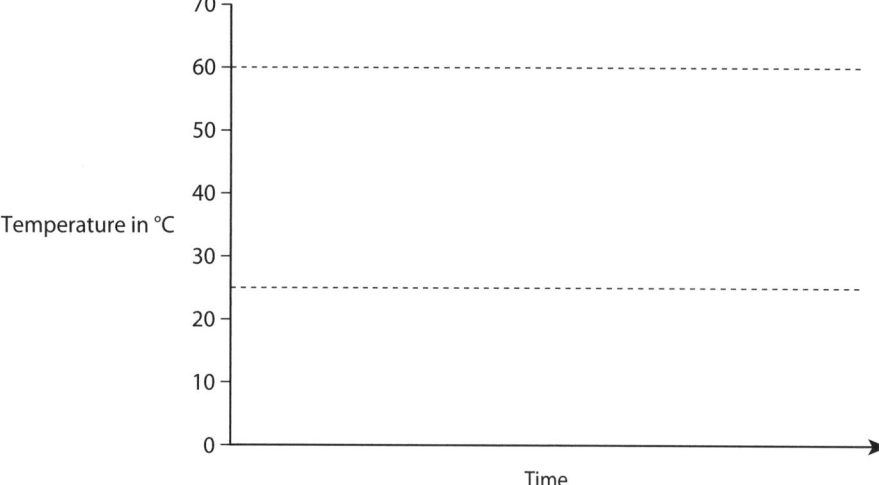

Exercise 3.4C Direction of thermal energy transfer 3

Challenge

In this exercise, you will make predictions about thermal energy transfer.

1   Zara's body temperature is 37 °C.

    a   Explain why Zara feels cold when the air temperature is 5 °C.

       ....

       ....

    b   Explain why Zara feels hot when the air temperature is 40 °C.

       ....

       ....

2   Arun fills a glass with water to drink.
The temperature of the water is 10 °C.

    Arun puts ice in the water. The temperature of the ice is −15 °C.

    Explain what will happen to the temperature of the water when the
ice is added.

    ....

    ....

    ....

3   Sofia makes a cup of hot coffee. She adds cold milk to the coffee.

    Explain what happens to the temperature of the coffee **and** the
temperature of the milk.

    ....

    ....

    ....

    ....

    ....

> 3.5 Ways of transferring thermal energy

Exercise 3.5A Describing thermal energy transfers

Focus

In this exercise, you will describe how thermal energy is transferred in different situations.

1   Complete the sentences using words from the list.
    Each word can be used more than once.

>   **conduction   convection   radiation**

a   Thermal energy is transferred from the Sun to Earth by ....

b   Thermal energy is transferred within metals by ....

c   When warm air rises through cold air, this is called ....

d   Neither .... nor .... can occur in
    a vacuum.

2   Draw straight lines to match the type of thermal energy transfer to
    the way it works.

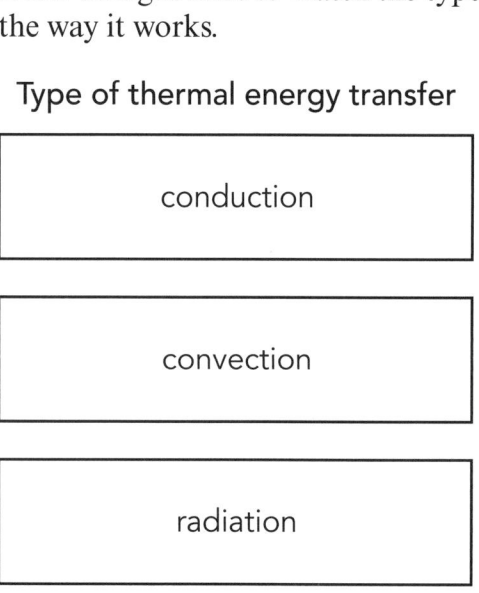

Type of thermal energy transfer

| conduction |
| convection |
| radiation |

How it works

| particles vibrate more, take up more space and decrease the density of the substance |
| particles vibrate more, collide with particles beside them, making these particles also vibrate more |
| type of wave that does not require particles to transfer thermal energy |

Exercise 3.5B Comparing thermal energy transfers

Practice

In this exercise, you will make comparisons between the three types of thermal energy transfer.

1   Explain why conduction of heat occurs more easily in solids than in gases.

    ....

    ....

    ....

2   Explain why convection can occur in liquids and gases but **not** in solids.

    ....

    ....

    ....

3   Explain why radiation can occur in a vacuum while conduction and convection **cannot** occur in a vacuum.

    ....

    ....

    ....

Exercise 3.5C Variables affecting thermal energy transfer

Challenge

In this exercise, you will consider the variables that affect thermal energy transfers.

Use ideas about conduction, convection or radiation when answering these questions.

1 **a** Explain why a cooking pot is made from metal.

....

....

 b Explain why the handle of the cooking pot is made from wood.

....

....

2 Explain why houses in hot countries are often painted white.

....

....

....

3 Explain why clothing made from wool can help you keep warm in cold weather.

....

....

....

4   A plastic box with shiny silver aluminium foil on the inside can be used to keep food hot.

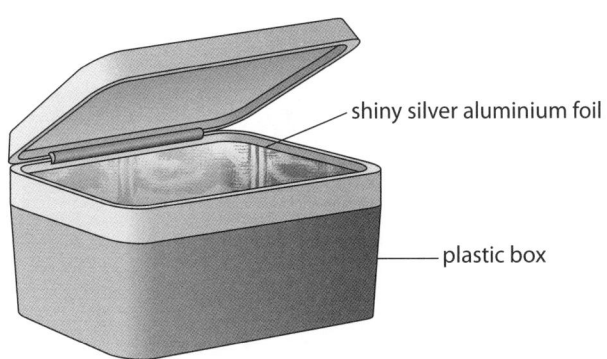

shiny silver aluminium foil

plastic box

Explain how this works.

....

....

....

....

....

> 3.6 Cooling by evaporation

Exercise 3.6A How evaporation works

Focus

In this exercise, you will think about what evaporation is and how it works.

1   Which of these describes evaporation?

Tick (✓) **one** box.

when a solid changes to a liquid   ☐

when a liquid changes to a gas   ☐

when a liquid changes to a solid   ☐

when a gas changes to a liquid   ☐

2 Which particles cause evaporation?

Tick (✓) **one** box.

The particles with the most energy. ☐

The particles with the least energy. ☐

Explain your answer.

....

....

3 The boiling point of water is 100 °C.

Zara: Water can evaporate at temperatures much lower than 100 °C

Sofia: Water can only evaporate at 100 °C

Zara

Sofia

Who is correct, Zara or Sofia? ....

Give an example to support your answer.

....

....

....

Exercise 3.6B Evaporation and cooling 1

Practice

In this exercise, you will think about how evaporation causes cooling.

1   Sweat is produced in the skin. Which of these explains how sweat can cool (lower the temperature of) the skin.

Tick (✓) **one** box.

Sweat evaporates, removing thermal energy from skin.   ☐

Sweat evaporates, adding thermal energy to the skin.   ☐

Sweat is produced at a lower temperature than the skin.   ☐

Sweat is produced at a higher temperature than the skin.   ☐

2   A liquid is evaporating. The liquid is **not** being heated.

    a   Explain what happens to the average energy of the particles in the liquid.

       ....

       ....

    b   Explain what happens to the temperature of the liquid.

       ....

       ....

3   Arun has sweat on his face. The air temperature is 25 °C. Arun uses a fan to blow air onto his face. The fan does **not** change the temperature of the air.

Explain why the fan helps Arun to cool (lose heat) faster.

....

....

....

Exercise 3.6C Evaporation and cooling 2

Challenge

In this exercise, you will think in more detail about how evaporation causes cooling.

1 Perfume evaporates faster than water.

Sofia has perfume and water at the same temperature.

Sofia puts an equal volume of the perfume and the water separately on her hand.

Explain which feels colder.

....

....

....

....

2 Humidity is a measure of the quantity of water vapour in air.
In conditions of high humidity, evaporation stops.

Explain why sweat will **not** cool (lower the temperature of) the skin in conditions of high humidity.

....

....

....

....

3   A type of air cooler works by blowing air from the room through
a sponge soaked in water.

Explain how blowing air through a sponge soaked in water lowers
the temperature of the air.

....

....

....

....

....

....

....

....

....

....

4 Maintaining life

> 4.1 Plants and water

Exercise 4.1A Water uptake by orange plant seedlings

Focus

In this exercise, you will use a set of results to make conclusions.

Scientists investigated root hairs on two varieties of orange plant seedlings, variety **A** and variety **B**.

They recorded:

- the mean numbers of root hairs per plant
- the mean length of the root hairs on each plant.

The table shows their results.

Orange plant variety	Mean number of root hairs per plant	Mean length of root hairs on each plant in mm
A	920	0.03
B	800	0.02

1   The scientists counted the number of root hairs on 10 plants of variety **A**.

   How could they use their results to calculate the mean number of root hairs per plant of variety **A**?

   ....

   ....

2   The scientists found that variety **A** orange plants took up more water in one hour than variety **B** orange plants.

Use the results in the table to explain why.

....

....

....

3   Describe what happens to water after it has been taken up by a root hair.

....

....

....

....

Exercise 4.1B Celery experiment

Practice

In this exercise, you will use a set of results to construct a line graph. You will use your graph to make a conclusion.

Zara investigates the rate of water movement up a celery stalk. She wants to find out how the temperature of the water affects this.

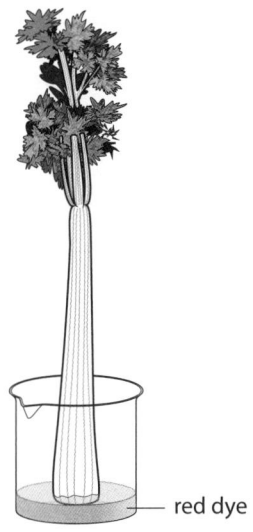

red dye

Zara takes eight celery stalks.

She stands each stalk in a beaker containing a red dye.

She puts each beaker into a water bath. Each water bath is kept at a different temperature.

After ten minutes she takes out all of the celery stalks.

She cuts each stalk across, every 0.5 cm along.

She looks for the red dye in each slice and estimates how far the dye has travelled through the slice.

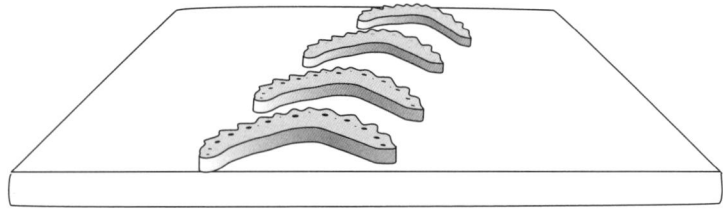

Zara records how far the dye has travelled up each stalk.
She writes her results in a table.

Temperature in °C	Distance the dye travels in cm
0	1.0
10	1.9
20	3.1
30	4.0
40	4.8
50	3.2
60	7.0
70	8.1

1   Which one of Zara's results is anomalous?
    (Anomalous means that it does not fit the pattern.)

    Draw a circle around the anomalous result in the table.

2 Use Zara's results to construct a line graph on the grid.

Put temperature in °C on the horizontal axis.

Put distance the dye travels in **cm** on the vertical axis.

Draw a line of best fit. Do not include the anomalous result.

3 What conclusion can Zara make from her experiment?

Tick (✓) **one** box.

Plants need more water when the temperature is higher. ☐

As temperature increases, the rate of transport of water in celery stalks increases. ☐

Celery leaves use water for photosynthesis. ☐

Exercise 4.1C Interpreting data about water uptake

Challenge

In this challenge task, you will look at some data collected by researchers who did experiments on wheat plants. You will choose a good way to display the data, and then make a suggestion, based on the data.

A team of scientists wanted to compare how much water is taken up by three different varieties of wheat growing in a cold place.

They grew seedlings of each of the three varieties of wheat.

They provided all of the seedlings with the same volume of water.

They placed the seedlings at a temperature of 2 °C.

They measured how much water each group of seedlings had taken up after two weeks, and again after six weeks.

The table shows the results.

Variety of wheat	Volume of water taken up per g of wheat plant, in cm³	
	after 2 weeks at 2 °C	after 6 weeks at 2 °C
A	78	102
B	64	94
C	72	122

1 Suggest why the scientists measured the volume of water taken up per gram of the wheat plants, rather than the volume taken up by a whole plant.

....

....

....

2 Think about different ways in which you could display these results.
Choose one good way and display the results on the grid.

3 Compare the volumes of water taken up by the three varieties of
wheat after two weeks.

....

....

....

4 Describe how the results after six weeks are different from those after two weeks.

....

....

....

5 Plants need to take up water so that they can photosynthesise and grow well.

Suggest which variety of wheat would be the best choice for a farmer in Canada, where the temperatures often fall very low.

Explain your choice.

....

....

....

> 4.2 Transpiration

Exercise 4.2 How temperature affects water loss

This exercise gives you practice in constructing results tables, drawing line graphs and dealing with anomalous results. You'll also do some calculations and use your knowledge to try to explain patterns in results.

Focus

Sofia set up an experiment to investigate this hypothesis:

Plants lose more water from their leaves when the temperature increases.

The diagrams show how Sofia set up her experiment.

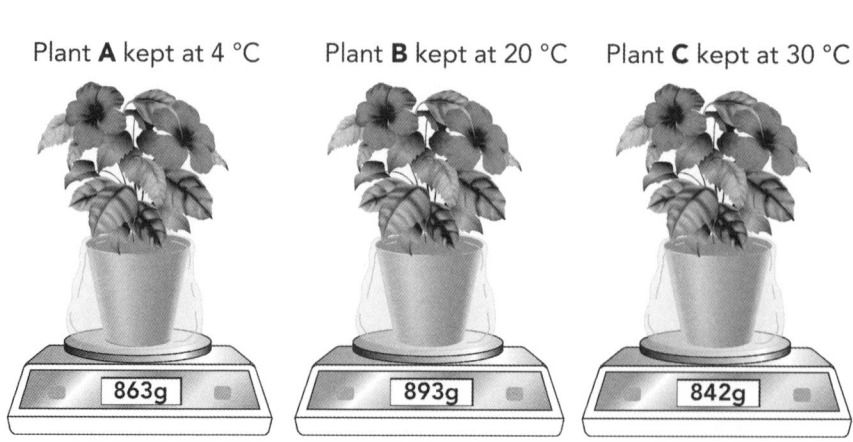

Plant **A** kept at 4 °C   Plant **B** kept at 20 °C   Plant **C** kept at 30 °C

863g   893g   842g

1   Look at Sofia's hypothesis.

Explain why she covered the pot and soil of each plant with a plastic bag.

....

....

....

2   Sofia read the mass, in grams, of each plant and pot each day for 8 days.

These are the results that she wrote down:

Plant **A**: 863, 854, 845, 837, 829, 822, 814, 807

Plant **B**: 893, 873, 856, 837, 861, 792, 779, 761

Plant **C**: 842, 810, 780, 748, 714, 682, 650, 618

Draw a results table, and fill in Sofia's results.

Practice

3   Sofia decided that one of her results was anomalous.
Draw a circle around the anomalous result in your results table.

4   Draw line graphs to display Sofia's results on the grid below.

Put time on the horizontal axis, and mass of plant and pot in grams on the vertical axis. You do not need to start at 0 on the *y*-axis.

Draw a separate line for each plant. What should you do about the anomalous result?

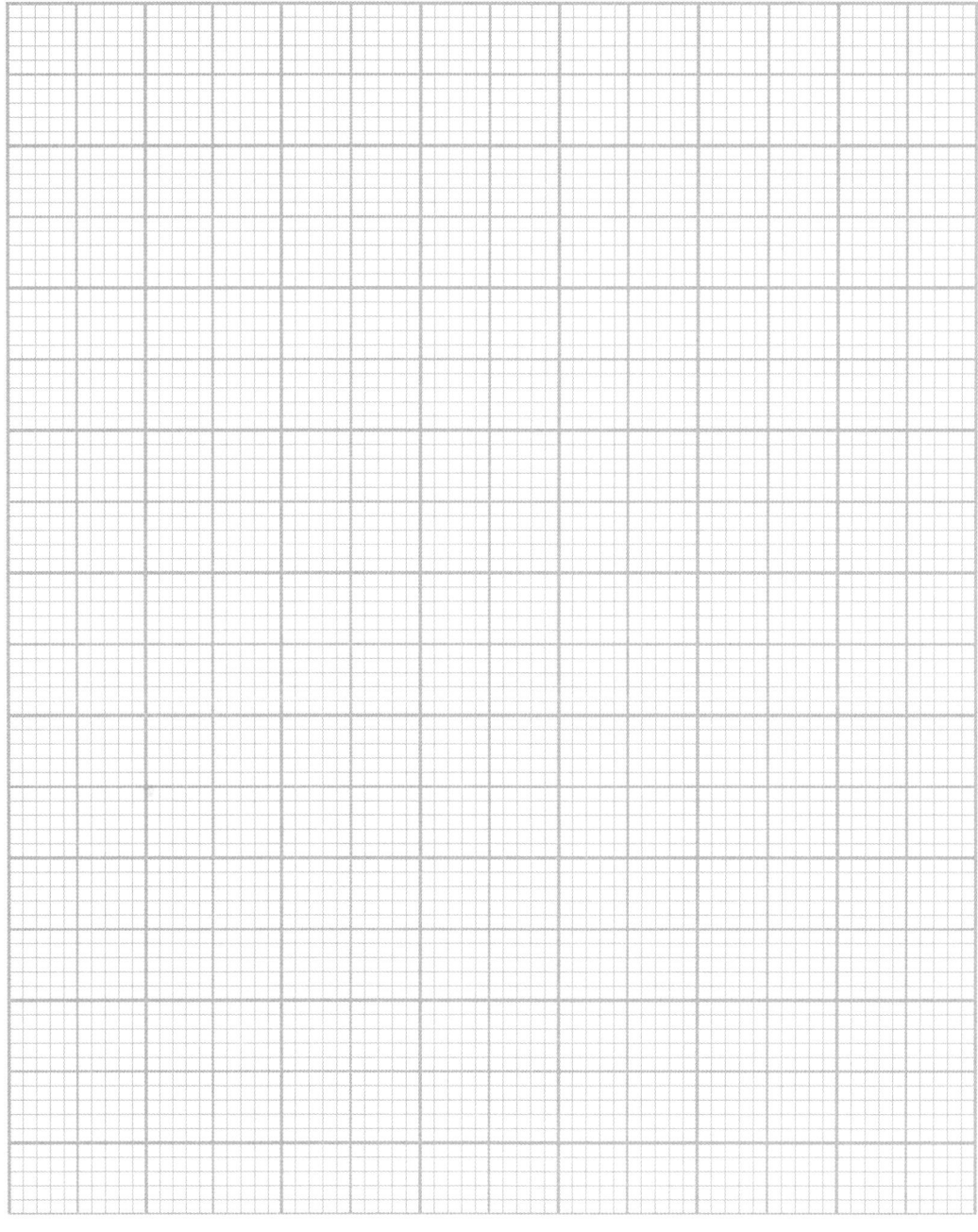

Challenge

5 Sofia calculated the mean loss of mass per day for plant **A** like this:

mass on day 1 = 863 g

mass on day 8 = 807 g

therefore loss of mass over 7 days was 863 − 807 = 56 g

therefore the mean loss of mass per day was 56 ÷ 7 = 8 g per day.

In the space below, calculate the mean loss of mass per day for plant **B** and for plant **C**.

mean for plant B = ... g per day

mean for plant C = ... g per day

6 Use your knowledge of plants and water to suggest an explanation for Sofia's results.

....

....

....

....

....

....

> 4.3 Excretion in humans

Exercise 4.3 Structure and function of the excretory system

In this exercise, you will check that you know the structure of the excretory system and can describe the functions of the different organs that are part of this system.

Focus

1 Complete the sentences. Use words from the list. Use each word once.

kidneys   renal   urea   urine   water

The .... are part of the excretory system.

This is also known as the .... system.

In the excretory system, a waste substance called .... is filtered out of the blood.

It dissolves in .... , forming a liquid called ....

Practice

2 Complete the diagram of the excretory system.

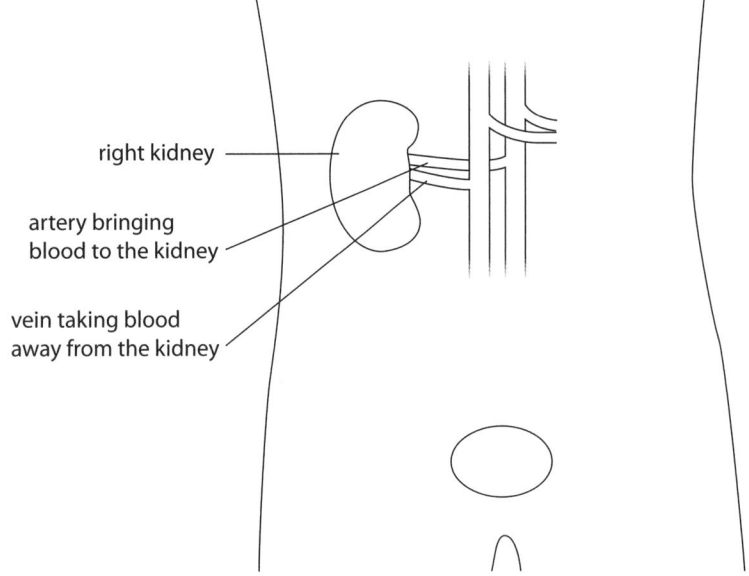

right kidney

artery bringing blood to the kidney

vein taking blood away from the kidney

3 Add labels to the diagram. You should label **four** other structures.

Challenge

4   Describe the function of each of the structures that you have
    labelled on the diagram.

....

....

....

....

....

....

....

> 4.4 Keeping a fetus healthy

Exercise 4.4A Length of pregnancy

Focus

In this exercise, you will practise organising data in the best way.
You will also think about the meaning of the word 'correlation',
and practise using data to support an argument.

The table shows the mean mass of an adult female of eight different species of mammal, and the mean time for which pregnancy lasts in that species.

Species	Mean mass of a female in kg	Mean length of pregnancy in days
moose (elk)	550	245
llama	113	330
goat	15	150
wolf	40	64
lion	150	108
rabbit	1	33
elephant	5000	640
chimpanzee	40	227

1 In the table below, rearrange the data so that it is easier to see if there is a relationship between the mean mass of a female and the mean length of pregnancy.

Species	Mean mass of a female in kg	Mean length of pregnancy in days

2   Is there a correlation between the mean mass of a female and the mean length of pregnancy? Explain your answer and use figures from the table to support it.

....

....

....

....

....

Exercise 4.4B Does caffeine affect birthweight?

Practice

In this exercise, you will look at some data collected by researchers in Sweden. You will practise using data to make conclusions and think about how an investigation could be improved.

A study was carried out in Sweden to investigate the idea that women who drink a lot of coffee during pregnancy might have smaller babies. 1037 pregnant women took part. They each answered a questionnaire about how much coffee they drank.

When their babies were born, their birthweights were measured. The results are shown in the table.

Mean caffeine intake per day in mg	Mean birthweight in g
less than 100	3660
100 to 299	3661
300 to 499	3597
500 or more	3694

1   Plot these results as a bar chart on the grid. Think carefully about the range for the scale on the vertical axis. Remember that you do not need to begin at 0.

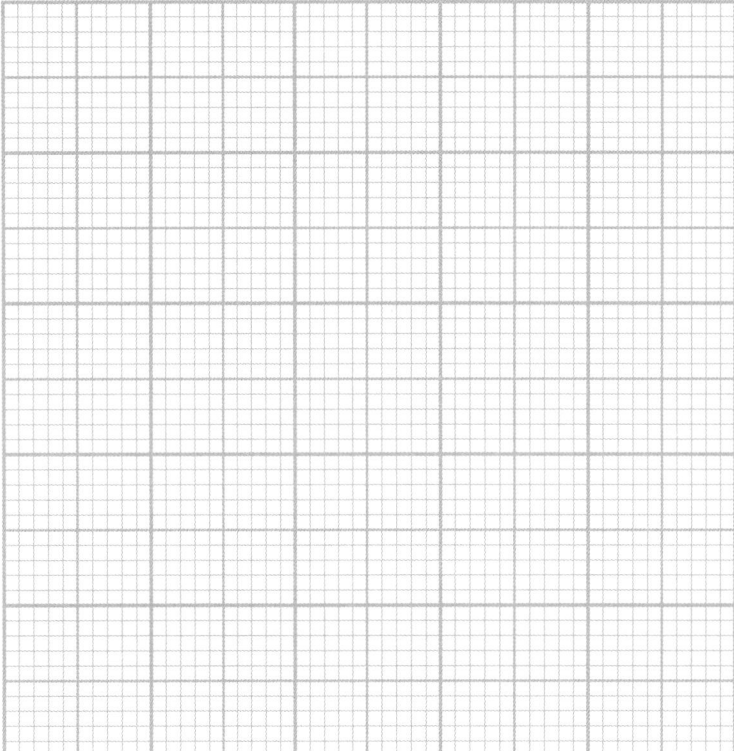

2   What conclusion can you make from these results? Explain your answer and use figures from the table to support it.

....

....

....

....

3   Suggest **two** ways in which the researchers could have improved their study.

....

....

....

....

Exercise 4.4C Smoking and birthweight

Challenge

In this exercise, you will analyse data about smoking and birthweight. You will use the data to draw conclusions and explain how you made these conclusions.

Scientists in Japan studied how the birthweight of a baby is affected if the mother smokes while she is pregnant.

They interviewed 53 386 mothers whose babies were born between 2004 and 2007 in a large city in Japan.

They asked the mothers whether they had smoked during pregnancy. They also recorded the mass of the baby at birth. If the baby's mass was less than 2500 g at birth, this was recorded as low birthweight.

The table shows their results.

Birth year	Mother smoked during pregnancy		Mother did not smoke during pregnancy	
	Number of babies born	Percentage of babies with low birthweight	Number of babies born	Percentage of babies with low birthweight
2004 to 2005	2609	14.0	23 713	9.6
2006 to 2007	2109	14.5	24 955	9.9

Look at the row for 2004 to 2005.

1 How many babies were born in total in 2004 to 2005?

....

2 Did most mothers smoke during pregnancy in 2004 to 2005? Use the numbers in the table to explain your answer.

....

....

....

....

3 Did smoking during pregnancy increase the risk of a baby having low birthweight? Use the numbers in the table to explain your answer.

....

....

....

....

Now look at the next row as well – the row for 2006 to 2007.

4 Look at the number of babies born. Is there any evidence that fewer women smoked during pregnancy in 2006 to 2007, than in 2004 to 2005? Use the numbers in the table to explain your answer.

....

....

....

....

5 Do you think that the results in the table prove that smoking during pregnancy is harmful to a fetus? Explain your answer.

....

....

....

....

....

5 ▶ Reactivity

› 5.1 Reactivity and displacement reactions

Exercise 5.1A Using the reactivity series

Focus

In this exercise, you will use the information from the reactivity series to make some predictions.

The diagram shows the reactivity series of metals.

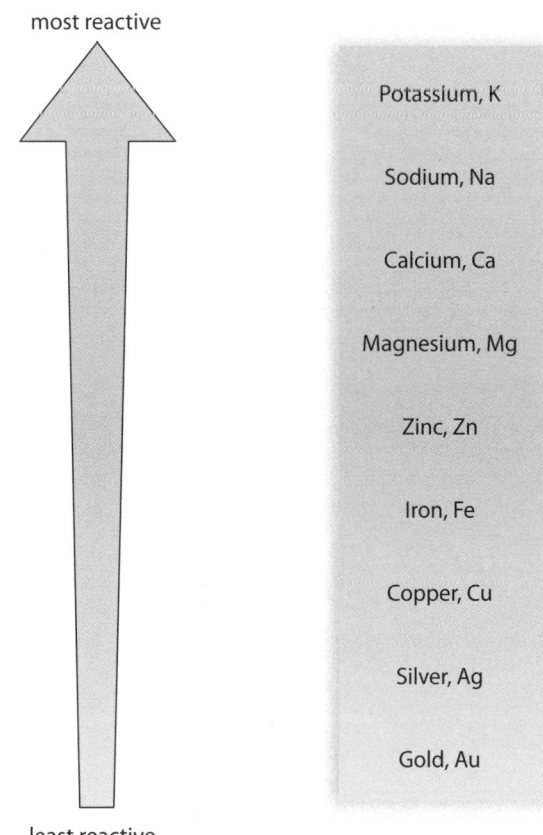

1 Sodium burns brightly when heated, and forms an oxide.
Does magnesium react **more vigorously** or **less vigorously** than sodium?

....

2 Copper reacts very slowly when heated.
Suggest how silver reacts when heated.

....

3 Iron reacts very slowly with dilute acid. How do you expect zinc to react with dilute acid, compared with iron?

....

....

4 If an iron nail is put in a solution of copper sulfate, there is a reaction. This is the word equation:

copper sulfate + iron → iron sulfate + copper

Iron is **more reactive** than copper, so it 'pushes out' or **displaces** the copper from the sulfate.

If you place a copper nail in a solution of iron sulfate, will there be a displacement reaction?

....

Explain your answer.

....

....

5 Suggest a metal that cannot displace copper in the solution of copper sulfate.

....

6 Metal X **displaces silver** in a solution of silver chloride.

Metal X **does not displace zinc** in a solution of zinc chloride.

Suggest what metal X could be. ....

7 Look at the possible reactions described below. Write **yes** next to those that will happen and **no** next to those that will not.

  a zinc and copper sulfate, to give copper ....

  b iron and magnesium chloride, to give magnesium ....

  c copper and zinc chloride, to give zinc ....

  d zinc and iron chloride, to give iron ....

  e iron and silver nitrate, to give silver ....

8 Write the word equation of the reaction between magnesium and zinc chloride.

.... + ... → .... + ...

Exercise 5.1B Displacement reactions

Practice

In this exercise, you will practise interpreting information and writing word equations.

1 More reactive metals can displace less reactive ones from solutions of salts. The table below shows the results of an experiment that uses displacement reactions.

	iron	copper	zinc	magnesium
copper sulfate	reaction		reaction	reaction
zinc sulfate	no reaction	no reaction		reaction
magnesium sulfate	no reaction	no reaction	no reaction	

  a The table shows that zinc displaces the copper in copper sulfate. What does this tell you about the reactivity of zinc and copper?

  ....

  b Write the word equation for the reaction between zinc and copper sulfate.

  ....

c The table shows there is no reaction between magnesium sulfate and zinc. What does this tell you about the reactivity of these two metals?

....

d Use the table to work out whether iron is more or less reactive than copper. Then, work out whether magnesium is more or less reactive than iron. Write these metals in order of reactivity, starting with the most reactive, based on the information in the table.

....

....

....

2 Sofia has been given the task of identifying a metal. She knows that the metal is one of zinc, iron, copper or silver. She has been given a number of small pieces of the metal and also some solutions of copper sulfate, zinc sulfate, iron sulfate and silver nitrate.

a Explain how she could use these solutions to identify the metal.

....

....

....

....

....

b Explain how you could use displacement reactions to distinguish between iron and zinc. You may use any solutions you choose.

....

....

....

....

....

Exercise 5.1C Displacing metals

Challenge

In this exercise, you will discuss the reactivity of metals and predict which displacement reactions will take place.

Arun has six metals **A**, **B**, **C**, **D**, **E** and **F**. He also has six test tubes of a solution of a salt of metal **A**, six test tubes of a solution of a salt of metal **B**, and so on. He adds a small piece of each metal to six tubes, one of each of the salt solutions.

The bar chart shows the number of displacement reactions that take place.

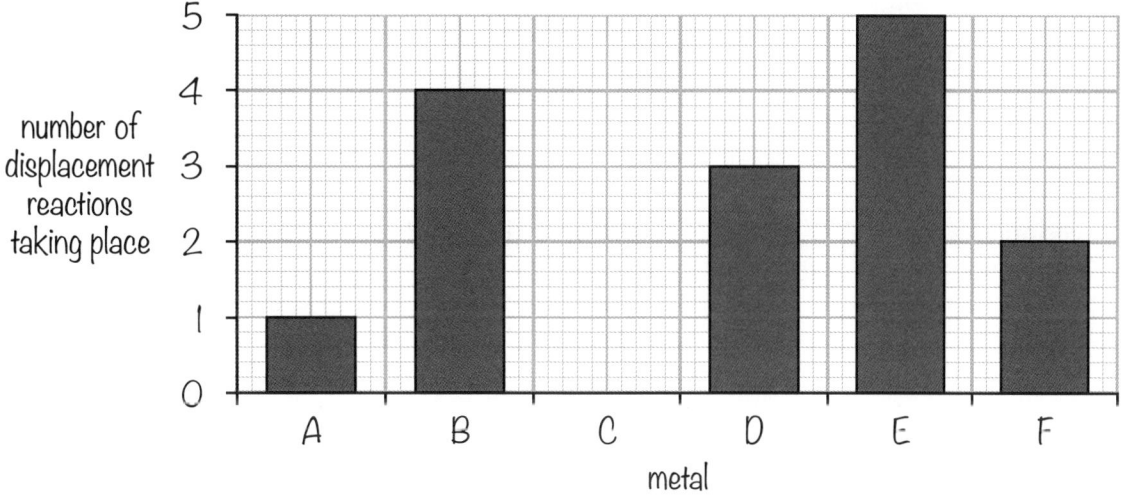

1   Which of the metals **A**, **B**, **C**, **D**, **E**, **F** is most reactive?
    Explain your choice.

    ....

    ....

    ....

2 Complete the table using Arun's results. Use a tick to show where a reaction happened and a cross where a reaction has not happened.

Start filling in the table for the most reactive metal first, then the next most reactive and so on.

		Metal					
		A	B	C	D	E	F
Metal salt	A						
	B						
	C						
	D						
	E						
	F						

3 Metal C is copper and metal D is zinc. Suggest what the other metals might be. Give reasons for your choices.

....

....

....

4 Complete the following word equations. If there is no reaction between the metal and the salt, write no reaction.

a copper sulfate + iron →...

b magnesium chloride + zinc →...

c iron sulfate + magnesium →...

d zinc chloride + silver →...

e zinc chloride + iron →...

5 Explain why it is not possible for you to carry out displacement reactions using the metal potassium.

....

....

> 5.2 Using the reactivity series and displacement reactions

Exercise 5.2 Using displacement reactions

Focus

This exercise will give you practice in using information from displacement reactions to identify an unknown metal.

1   A metal displaces the iron from a solution of iron sulfate and the copper from a solution of copper sulfate. This metal does not displace the magnesium from a solution of magnesium sulfate.

   a   What does this tell you about the reactivity of the unknown metal?

   ....

   ....

   b   This unknown metal could be one of two metals shown in the reactivity list in Exercise 5.1A. Which two?

   ....

   c   Name a metal that you could use to:

   displace copper from copper sulfate ....

   displace zinc from zinc chloride ....

Practice

In this exercise, you will practise describing and explaining the use of displacement reactions.

2 **a** Explain why zinc can be used to displace iron from iron chloride.

....

....

b Write the word equation for the reaction that takes place when zinc reacts with iron chloride.

....

c Copper is less reactive than iron. Predict whether zinc can be used to displace copper from copper chloride.

....

d Explain why magnesium cannot be displaced by zinc in a solution of magnesium chloride.

....

....

Challenge

In this exercise you will explain how displacement reactions are used in practical ways.

3 **a** Explain how the displacement of iron from iron oxide is used to weld rails together.

....

....

....

....

b Why is this method used and not other methods of welding?

....

....

c Write the word equation for this reaction.

4 Iron is produced from its ore, iron oxide, by using a displacement reaction. This is done in a blast furnace.

a Which element is used to displace iron?

....

b Describe briefly how this process is carried out.

....

....

....

c Write the word equation for this reaction.

d Suggest where the element used in this reaction fits in the reactivity series.

....

> 5.3 Salts

Exercise 5.3A Which acid is used to make which salt?

Focus

In this exercise, you will identify which acid is used to produce a salt.
Then you identify a salt from its formula.

1   Link the name of the acid with its formula, and with the name
    of the salt it produces.

    Draw lines to link the boxes. Use a ruler.

Acid	Formula	Salt
hydrochloric acid	HNO_3	sulfates
sulfuric acid	HCl	nitrates
nitric acid	H_2SO_4	chlorides

2   The following compounds are all salts of magnesium. For each one,
    state the acid that has been used to make the salt.

    •   magnesium chloride ....

    •   magnesium sulfate ....

    •   magnesium nitrate ....

3   Write the name of the salt next to its formula.

    •   NaCl ....

    • $CuSO_4$ ....

    • $CuCl_2$ ....

    • KNO_3 ....

4   Citric acid is found in fruit. What are salts of this acid called?

    ....

Exercise 5.3B Making salts

Practice

In this exercise, you will explain how some salts are made and practise some word equations.

1   Explain how you could make the salt zinc nitrate using zinc metal.

....

....

....

....

2   Write the word equation for this reaction.

....

3   Explain why you could not make silver sulfate by that method.

....

....

4   Explain why you could not make potassium sulfate by that method.

....

....

5   Copper sulfate is made by mixing copper oxide with sulfuric acid and gently heating it.

   a   Why is it important that the acid mixture does not boil?

....

....

   b   Write the word equation for the reaction.

....

6 Write the word equations for the following reactions:

a magnesium and nitric acid

....

b copper oxide and nitric acid

....

c zinc and hydrochloric acid

....

d zinc and sulfuric acid

....

Exercise 5.3C Practical steps for making salts

Challenge

In this exercise, you will describe in detail the practical steps needed to produce a salt using an oxide and an acid.

1 Why is copper chloride not made by reacting copper with dilute sulfuric acid?

....

....

2 Describe the three steps involved in producing crystals of the salt copper chloride. For each step, describe the method and include the safety precautions needed. Use diagrams if they help your answer.

....

....

....

....

....

....

....

....

....

....

....

....

....

....

....

....

....

....

....

....

> 5.4 Other ways of making salts

Exercise 5.4A Preparing copper chloride

Focus

In this exercise, you will explain the steps in the formation of a salt. You will also consider some of the safety precautions needed.

Zara and Sofia are preparing the salt copper chloride. Zara pours some hydrochloric acid into a beaker. Then Sofia adds some copper carbonate.

1 What happens when Sofia adds the copper carbonate to the acid?

....

....

Sofia adds more and more copper carbonate until there is no more reaction. There is some unreacted copper carbonate left in the beaker. Sofia filters the mixture.

filtrate

2 What is left in the filter paper?

....

3 The filtrate passes through the filter paper into the flask. What is this liquid?

....

4 Next, Zara and Sofia want to produce crystals of the salt. What must they do?

....

....

5   Why must they be very careful when they carry out this step?

....

....

6   What should they do to reduce the hazard?

....

....

....

7   Write the word equation for this reaction.

copper
carbonate +   →   +   +

Exercise 5.4B Preparing potassium chloride

Practice

In this exercise, you will describe the steps needed in some practical
work to produce a salt from an acid and an alkali.

Zara and Marcus want to prepare the salt potassium chloride,
using potassium hydroxide.

1   Which acid should they use?

....

2   For the first step in this process, Zara and Marcus put $20\,cm^3$
of potassium hydroxide in a conical flask. They use the acid to
neutralise it.

List the equipment they will need for this first step in the process.

....

....

....

....

....

3 Describe the method for carrying out this step.
Include any safety precautions.

....

....

....

....

....

....

....

....

4 How will they know when the potassium hydroxide is neutralised?

....

....

5 When the potassium hydroxide is neutralised, Zara and Marcus
have a coloured solution. How do they remove the colour, so that
the crystals of potassium chloride are pure?

....

....

....

6 Write the word equation for the neutralisation reaction.

7 Write the symbol equation for this reaction.

Exercise 5.4C Mystery substances

Challenge

In this exercise, you will use the information given to identify some substances.

Arun and Marcus had three different substances, **A**, **B** and **C** each in the form of powder.

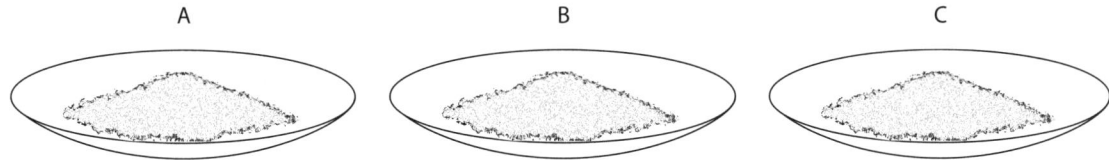

They placed a sample of each in one of three different test tubes.

They added a **different** liquid to each test tube.

They observed the reactions and did some tests.

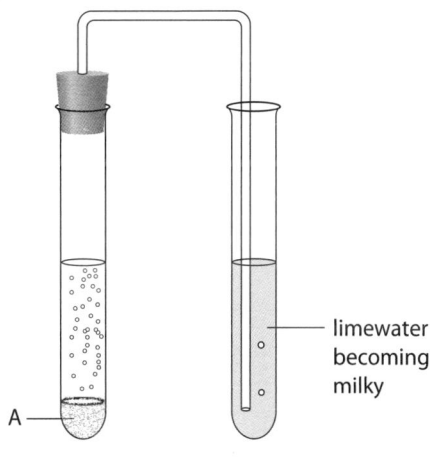

In the tube containing **A**, bubbles of gas were produced. When this gas was passed through limewater, it became milky.

limewater becoming milky

In the tube containing **B**, no bubbles were produced.

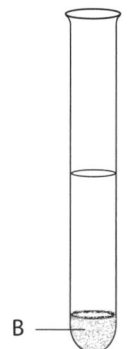

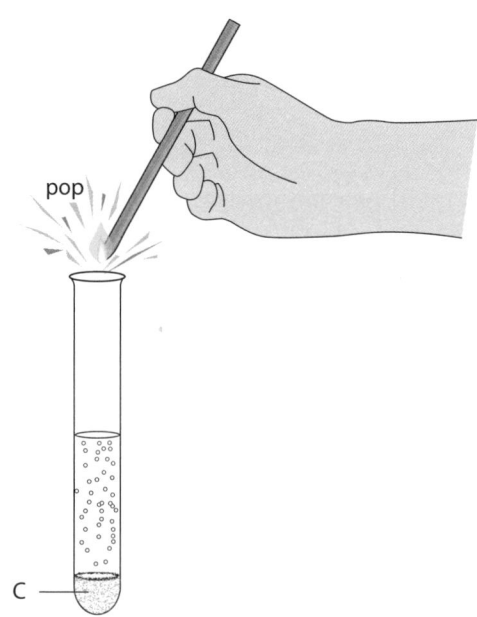

In the tube containing **C**, bubbles of gas were produced. When the students collected this gas and tested it with the lighted splint, there was a squeaky pop.

After these substances had finished reacting, Arun and Marcus heated the three solutions (after filtering where necessary). They evaporated the substances to dryness to form three crystalline substances:

substance **A** produced **zinc sulfate**

substance **B** produced **iron chloride**

substance **C** produced **magnesium chloride**.

1   Which gas did substance **A** produce?

    ....

2   Which gas did substance **C** produce?

    ....

3   Which general name is given to the crystalline substances produced in this way, after evaporation?

    ....

4   Suggest which liquid was added to tube A.

    ....

5   Suggest which liquid was added to tube B.

    ....

6   Suggest which liquid was added to tube C.

....

7   Suggest what substance **A** could have been.

....

8   Suggest what substance **B** could have been.

....

9   Suggest what substance **C** could have been.

....

10   Write a word equation for the reaction involving substance **A**.

....

11   Write a word equation for the reaction involving substance **B**.

....

12   Write a word equation for the reaction involving substance **C**.

....

> 5.5 Rearranging atoms

Exercise 5.5A What happens to the atoms and the mass when chemicals react?

Focus

In this exercise, you will develop your understanding of how atoms rearrange in a chemical reaction and look at what happens to the mass of products in a reaction.

When chemicals react together, none of the atoms is lost. They rearrange to make other chemicals.

1   In forming magnesium oxide, one atom of magnesium bonds with
     one atom of oxygen.

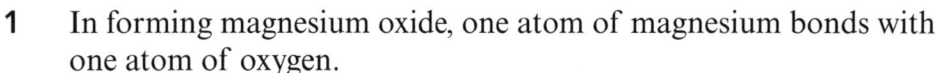

magnesium   +   oxygen   →   magnesium oxide

Colour the atoms of magnesium green.
Colour the atoms of oxygen red.

2   This diagram shows magnesium and hydrochloric acid reacting.

magnesium + hydrochloric acid →   + hydrogen

   a   Colour the atoms of magnesium green.
        Colour the atoms of chlorine yellow.

   b   Name the salt that is produced.

        ....

3   a   In the reaction shown in question 2, how many:

        atoms of hydrogen are on the left side of the equation?........................

        atoms of hydrogen are on the right side of the equation? ....

        atoms of chlorine are on the left side of the equation? ....

        atoms of chlorine are on the right side of the equation? ....

   b   Are there the same number of magnesium atoms on each side

        of the equation?........................

4   Now look at this reaction.

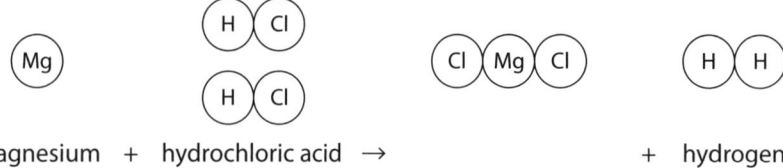

oxygen   +   hydrogen   →   water

   a   Colour the atoms of oxygen red. Leave the hydrogen atoms blank.

b Draw a circle around the word or words to make this statement correct:

The number of hydrogen atoms in the reactants is **larger than / smaller than / the same as** the number of hydrogen atoms in the products.

c Write a statement about the number of oxygen atoms in the reactants and in the products.

....

5 Marcus places 10 g of iron filings in a test tube. He adds 6 g of sulfur and mixes the two powders. He then heats the mixture.

The iron and sulfur react together to form iron sulfide.

When the reaction is complete the mass of the product is 16 g. The mass **does not change**.

Zara puts 15 g of iron filings and 9 g of sulfur in her test tube and heats it.

What is the mass of Zara's product? .... g

6 Zara now adds 30 g of calcium carbonate to 50 g hydrochloric acid in a 250 cm³ beaker.

What does Zara expect the reading on the top pan balance to be when the reaction has finished?

....

Exercise 5.5B Before and after the reaction

Practice

This exercise will help you to understand and explain what happens to atoms in a chemical reaction and explain some unexpected results.

1   The products of a chemical reaction contain the elements calcium, chlorine, hydrogen, oxygen and carbon.

   What elements were present in the reactants?

   ....

   ....

2   The particle diagram shows the reactants in a chemical reaction. Complete the word and symbol equations and draw a particle diagram for the missing product.

   sulfur   +   oxygen   →   ....

   S   + O_2 →   ....

3   This is the word equation for the reaction of magnesium carbonate with hydrochloric acid.

   magnesium carbonate + hydrochloric acid → magnesium chloride + carbon dioxide + water

   a   Which elements are present in magnesium carbonate?

   ....

   b   Which elements are present in carbon dioxide?

   ....

   c   Water contains the elements hydrogen and oxygen. Where did the hydrogen in the water come from in this reaction?

   ....

   d   Where did the chlorine in the magnesium chloride come from in this reaction?

   ....

4   If the mass of the products in the reaction above was 45 g, what was the mass of the reactants?

....

5   When magnesium reacts with sulfuric acid, the products are magnesium sulfate and hydrogen.

If there are 25 g of magnesium at the start of the reaction how much magnesium will be present in the magnesium sulfate?

....

6   Explain what is meant by the term conservation of mass.

....

....

Arun is investigating the idea of conservation of mass.

•   He places some zinc in a beaker and finds the mass of the zinc.

•   He places some dilute sulfuric acid in a beaker and finds the mass of the sulfuric acid.

•   He then mixes the zinc metal and the sulfuric acid in another beaker.

•   When the reaction has finished, he finds the mass of the contents of the beaker.

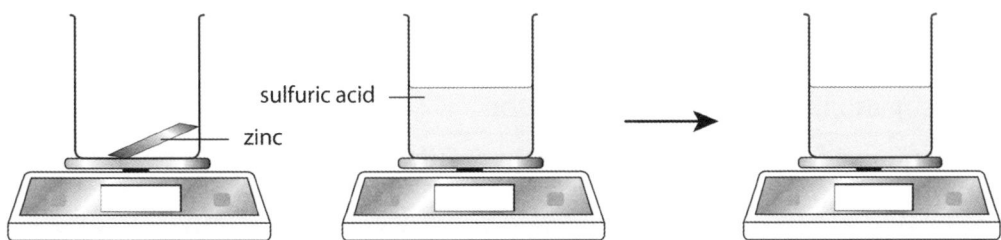

Arun starts with 100 g zinc and 150 g sulfuric acid.

7   What is the mass of the products of this reaction?

....

8   Write the word equation for this reaction.

....

9 At the end of the reaction, Arun finds that the mass of the contents of the beaker is 247 g. He repeats the experiment and gets the same result.

a   Has he made a mistake?

    ....

b   Suggest why Arun got this result.

    ....

    ....

10 When a scientist gets an unexpected result in an experiment what should they do?

    ....

    ....

    ....

Exercise 5.5C Investigating burning magnesium

Challenge

In this exercise, you will make a conclusion from experimental data and consider the practical problems when carrying out an investigation.

In an investigation, magnesium is burned in a limited volume of pure oxygen. The aim of the investigation is to answer this question.

How does the mass of the compound formed depend on the mass of the magnesium burned?

1 What variables need to be controlled to make this investigation fair?

    ....

    ....

2 Write the word equation for the reaction between magnesium and oxygen.

    ....

lid

deflagrating spoon

gas jar containing oxygen

magnesium ribbon

These results were obtained.

Mass of magnesium burned in g	Mass of compound formed in g
0.5	0.9
1.0	1.8
1.5	2.6
2.0	3.4
2.5	3.4
3.0	3.4

3 Plot the results on the grid below. Join the points appropriately.

4 State a **conclusion** you can make from these data.

....

....

5 Explain why the mass of the compound formed stays the same when the mass of the magnesium used increases from 2.0 g to 3.0 g.

....

....

6 If you carried out this investigation in a laboratory, suggest:

a problems you could have getting accurate results

....

....

....

....

....

....

b safety aspects you should consider.

....

....

....

....

....

....

6 ▶ Sound and space

> 6.1 Loudness and pitch of sound

Exercise 6.1A Comparing sound waves

Focus

In this exercise, you will compare sound waveforms as they are seen on an oscilloscope screen.

Zara plays four different notes on the flute.

The diagram shows how the four waveforms from these notes appear on an oscilloscope screen.

You can refer to each wave once, more than once or not at all.

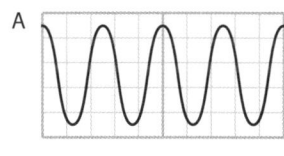

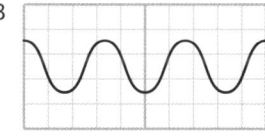

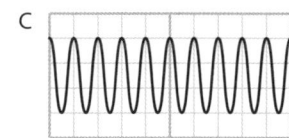

1   Which is the loudest sound? ....

2   Which has the largest amplitude? ....

3   Which is the quietest sound? ....

4   Which is the highest pitch sound? ....

5   Which is the lowest pitch sound? ....

6   Which has the highest frequency? ....

Exercise 6.1B Drawing sound waves

Practice

In this exercise, you will draw sound waveforms as they appear on oscilloscope screens using your understanding of amplitude and frequency.

This diagram shows the waveform of a sound.

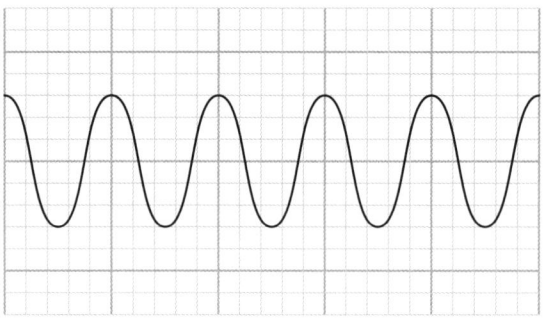

1   On this blank grid, draw how the waveform appears when:

   • the amplitude increases

   • the frequency stays the same.

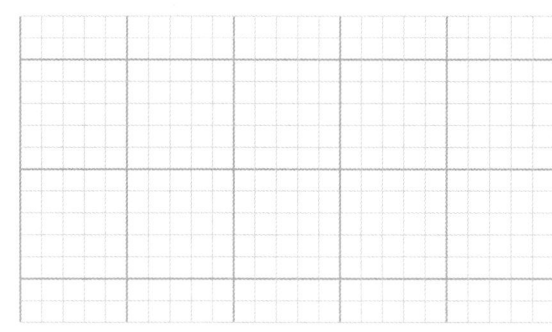

2   On this blank grid, draw how the waveform appears when:

   • the frequency increases

   • the amplitude stays the same.

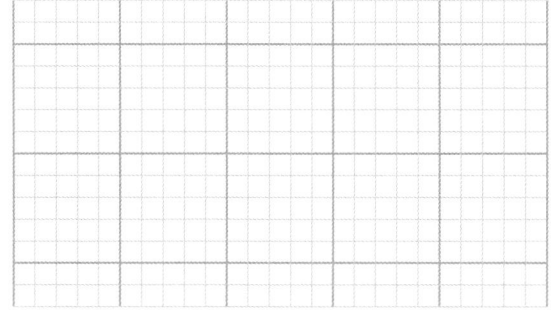

3   On this blank grid, draw how the waveform appears when:

   • the amplitude decreases

   • the frequency decreases.

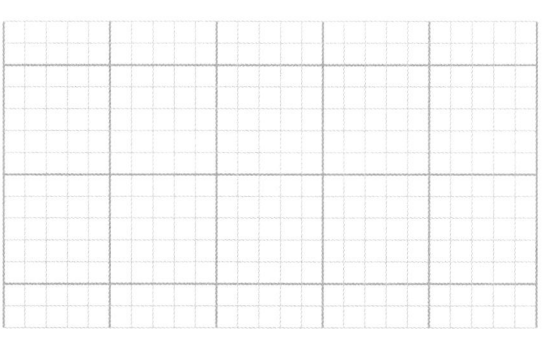

Exercise 6.1C Understanding sound waves

Challenge

In this exercise, you will show your understanding of amplitude and frequency in sound waves.

1   A sound wave travels through air.

  The sound wave makes the particles in air move forward by 0.5 mm. After the particles return to their original position, they move backward by 0.5 mm.

  The particles make 250 complete vibrations in 1 second.

  a   State the amplitude of this sound wave.

  .... mm

  b   State the frequency of this sound wave.

  Give the unit of frequency with your answer.

  .... unit ....

2   A sound wave has an amplitude of 0.1 mm and a frequency of 1200 Hz.
  The sound wave changes to have an amplitude of 0.04 mm and a frequency of 1500 Hz.

  Describe **two** ways that the sound changes.

  ....

  ....

  ....

  ....

3   Arun plays a musical note on the guitar by plucking a string.

Arun plays a second musical note that is double the frequency of the first note.

Describe how each of these changes between the first and second notes affect the:

a   sound produced by the string

....

b   vibrations of the guitar string

....

c   vibrations of the air particles caused by the string.

....

> 6.2 Interference of sound

Exercise 6.2A Reinforcing sound

Focus

In this exercise, you will think about what happens when sound waves reinforce.

1   What happens when a sound is reinforced?
Tick (✓) **one** box.

The sound becomes higher pitched. ☐   The sound becomes lower pitched. ☐

The sound becomes louder. ☐   The sound becomes quieter. ☐

2   The diagram represents two sound waves that meet each other.

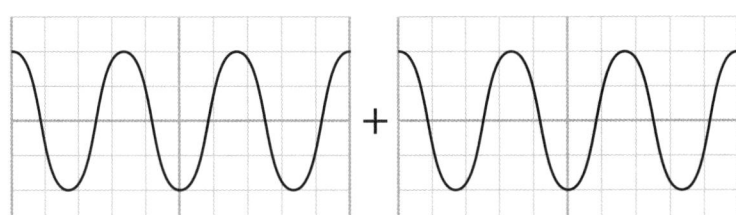

Which diagram shows the result when these two waves meet?
Circle the correct answer.

A

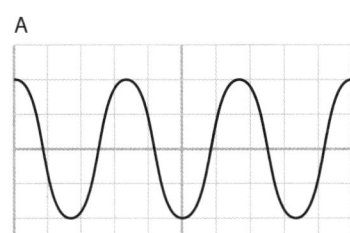

B

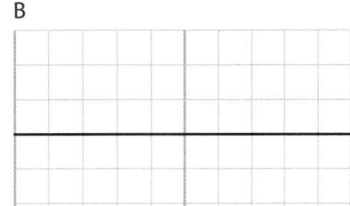

C

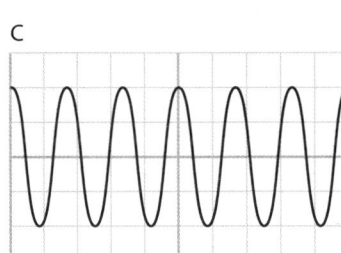

D

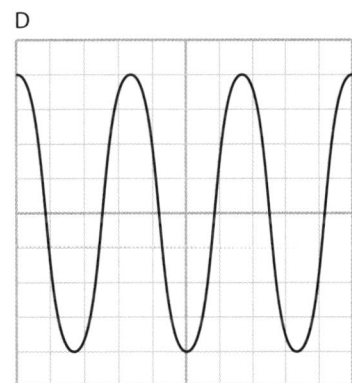

3   Zara and Sofia both play a piano in the same room.
Zara and Sofia both play the same note at the same time.

Why does this note sound louder than notes they play separately?

Tick (✓) **one** box.

The sound waves reinforce.   ☐

The sound waves cancel.   ☐

The sound waves make a higher pitch.   ☐

The sound waves make a lower pitch.   ☐

Exercise 6.2B Cancelling and reinforcing

Practice

In this exercise, you will think about how sound waves can cancel or reinforce each other.

1   Arun listens to the sound of one musical note from a loudspeaker.

    a   Another identical note reinforces the sound from the loudspeaker.

        State any difference in pitch and loudness that Arun hears when these sound waves reinforce.

        The pitch ....

        The loudness ....

    b   Another sound of the same pitch cancels the sound from the loudspeaker.

        Describe what Arun hears.

        ....

        ....

2   The diagram represents a sound wave, S.

Wave S

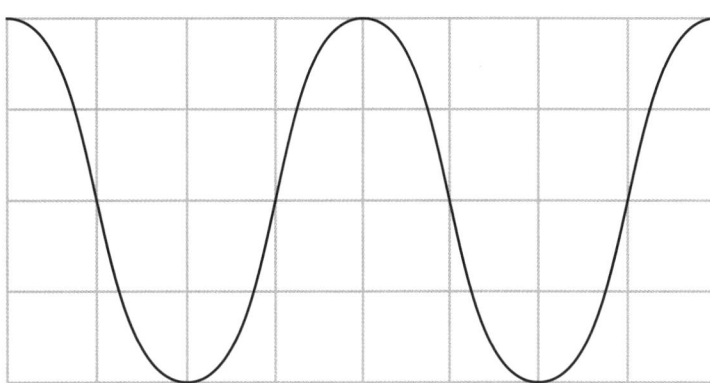

a   On this grid, draw another wave
     that would reinforce wave S.

b   On this grid, draw another wave
     that would cancel wave S.

Exercise 6.2C Interfering sound waves

Challenge

In this exercise, you will think about what must happen for sound waves to reinforce or cancel.

1 a Two sound waves, A and B, meet and reinforce. Sounds A and B have the same pitch.

The resulting wave, C, has double the amplitude of one of these waves.

    i State how the amplitudes of waves A and B compare to each other.

        ....

    ii State how the frequencies of waves A and B compare to each other.

        ....

    iii State how the frequency of wave C compares to the frequency of wave A.

        ....

b Two other sound waves, D and E, meet and cancel each other completely.

State how the amplitudes and frequencies of waves D and E compare before they meet.

Amplitudes

....

Frequencies

....

2 The diagram shows the vibration of a particle, P, in air.

A sound wave, W, is making the particle vibrate.

Particle P vibrates with a frequency of 2500 Hz.

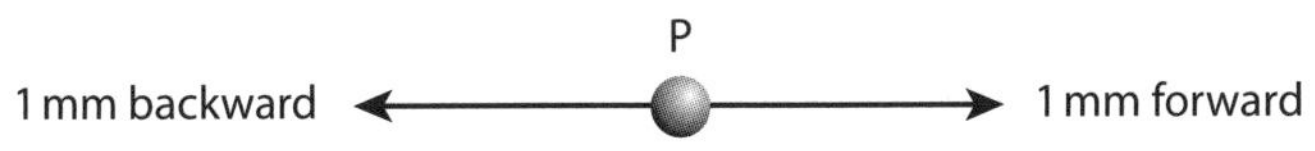

P

1 mm backward ← ——————●—————— → 1 mm forward

a Another sound wave, S, with the same amplitude and
frequency meets sound wave W. The two sound waves
reinforce each other to give a wave with double the amplitude.

    i   State the frequency of vibration of P when the two waves
reinforce.

       ....

    ii   State the amplitude of vibration of P when the two waves
reinforce.

       ....

b The sound making wave S stops. Wave W continues and
particle P vibrates as shown in the diagram.

Another sound wave, Q, meets wave W.
The result is that both waves cancel.

State the frequency and amplitude of wave Q.

Frequency: ....

Amplitude: ....

> 6.3 Formation of the Moon

Exercise 6.3A How was the Moon formed?

Focus

In this exercise, you will think about how the Moon was formed.

1   The diagrams show stages suggested by the collision theory for the formation of the Moon.

   The diagrams are **not** in the correct order.

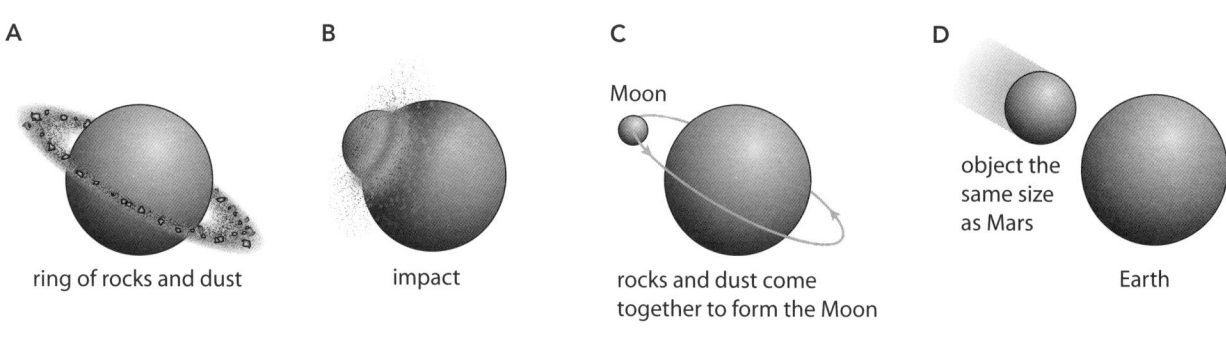

A   ring of rocks and dust

B   impact

C   Moon   rocks and dust come together to form the Moon

D   object the same size as Mars   Earth

   Write the letters of the diagrams to show the correct order of the events in the collision theory.

   1 .... **2** .... **3** .... **4** ....

2   The collision theory for the formation of the Moon describes an object the same size as Mars.
   What was this object?
   Tick (✓) **one** box.

   An asteroid.   ☐

   A newly formed star.   ☐

   A newly formed planet.   ☐

   A comet from outside the Solar System.   ☐

3   In the collision theory, the object that collided with Earth was
    called Theia. If the collision theory were correct, which object
    would contain particles from Theia?

    Tick (✓) **one** box.

    The Moon only.   ☐

    The Earth only.   ☐

    Both the Earth and the Moon.   ☐

    Neither the Earth nor the Moon.   ☐

Exercise 6.3B Describing the collision theory

Practice

In this exercise, you will describe the collision theory for the formation
of the Moon.

1   The diagram shows a timeline of the Solar System. The timeline
    starts when the Solar System was first formed and continues to the
    present day. The timeline covers 4600 million years.

    Which arrow shows the time of the formation of the Moon
    according to the collision theory?

    Write the letter: ....

2 Describe how the Moon was formed according to the collision theory.
You can use the space to draw a diagram if that helps your answer.

....

....

....

....

....

....

....

....

Exercise 6.3C Evidence for the collision theory

Challenge

In this exercise, you will consider evidence for the collision theory of the Moon's formation.

1 List **three** pieces of evidence that support the collision theory.

1 ....

....

2 ....

....

3 ....

....

2 Give **one** piece of evidence that contradicts the collision theory.

....

....

3 Another theory for the formation of the Moon is the fission theory. The fission theory suggests that the Earth and Moon were once the same object. This object then split into two parts soon after formation. The two parts are now the Earth and the Moon.

Which piece of evidence could support **both** the fission theory **and** the collision theory?

Tick (✓) **one** box.

The composition of rocks on the Moon is very similar to that on Earth. ☐

The Moon is smaller than the Earth. ☐

The Earth only has one moon and some other planets have more than one moon. ☐

The moons of Mars were originally asteroids. ☐

4 A different theory for the origin of the Moon is called the capture theory. The capture theory suggests that:

- the Moon was an object that was formed separately and far away from Earth
- this object was passing close by Earth
- the object was attracted by gravity from the Earth
- the object then remained in orbit around the Earth.

a State **one** piece of evidence that supports the collision theory but contradicts the capture theory.

....

....

b Explain how your answer to part **a** supports the collision theory but contradicts the capture theory.

....

....

....

....

> 6.4 Nebulae

Exercise 6.4A What are nebulae?

Focus

In this exercise, you will think about what nebulae are.

1   Arrange these objects in order of size from smallest to largest.

               star   **nebula**   **moon**   **asteroid**

....

2   Which statements about nebulae are true?

Tick (✓) **all** correct statements.

All nebulae contain dust and gas. ☐

All nebulae act as stellar nurseries. ☐

All nebulae are different shapes. ☐

All nebulae are bigger than the Milky Way galaxy. ☐

3   Name the gas that is most commonly found in nebulae.

....

Exercise 6.4B Types of nebula

Practice

In this exercise, you will compare different types of nebula.

The table contains information about four different types of nebula.

Type of nebula	Example	Information about this type of nebula
emission nebula	Orion Nebula	emit a large quantity of energy, so they appear bright against the background of space
dark nebula	Horsehead Nebula	block the light from stars that are behind them, so they appear almost black
reflection nebula	Pleiades	only reflect the light from nearby stars, so they can appear very bright
supernova remnant	Crab Nebula	emit a very large quantity of energy for a relatively short time, so they can appear as some of the brightest objects in the sky

Use information in the table to answer these questions.

1   Name one type of nebula that emits its own light.

....

2   Name one example of a nebula that does not emit its own light.

....

3   **a**   Suggest one type of nebula that could act as a stellar nursery.

....

   b   Explain your answer.

....

....

....

Exercise 6.4C Stellar nurseries

Challenge

In this exercise, you will consider what happens in stellar nurseries.

1 Describe what is meant by the term stellar nursery.

....

....

2 Briefly describe how a star is formed.

....

....

....

....

3 Scientists have estimated the numbers of stars that have been formed since the Universe began. The number of stars that are formed in each time period is called the star formation rate.

The graph shows the results of these estimates.

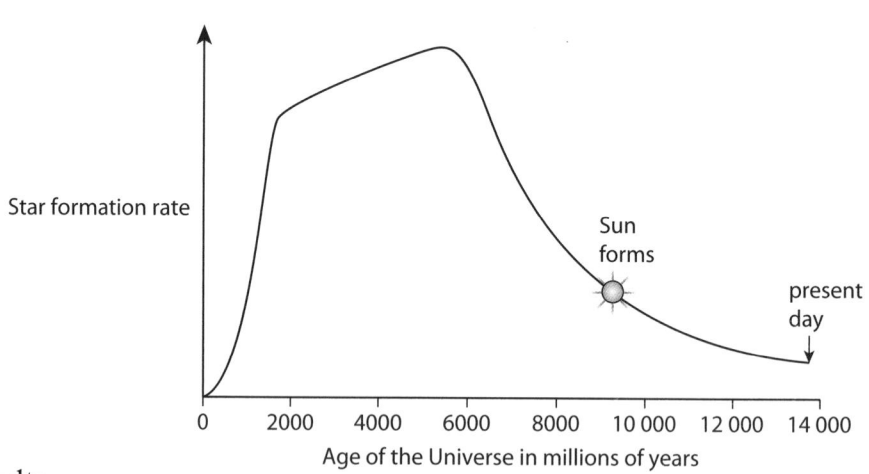

Describe the trends in the results.

....

....

....

....

....

› 6.5 Tectonics

Exercise 6.5A Movement of tectonic plates

Focus

In this exercise, you will think about how tectonic plates move.

1   The diagram shows a section through part of the Earth.

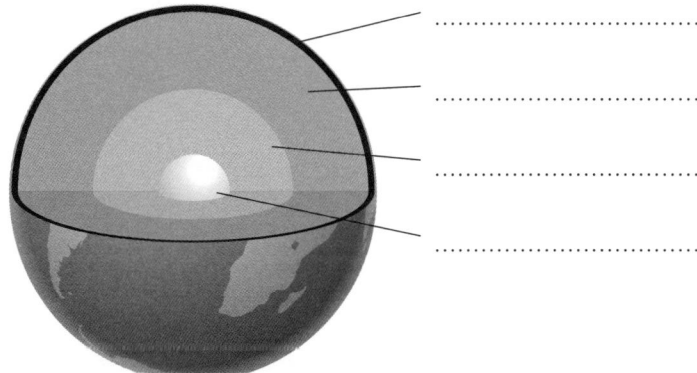

       ....

       ....

       ....

       ....

   a   Add labels to the diagram. Use the words:

           mantle   **inner core**   **crust**   **outer core**

   b   Draw arrows on the diagram to show the direction of
   convection currents inside the Earth.

   c   Which of the layers that you labelled in part **a** is made of
   tectonic plates?

       ....

2 The diagram shows how scientists think some of the continents may have looked about 200 million years ago.

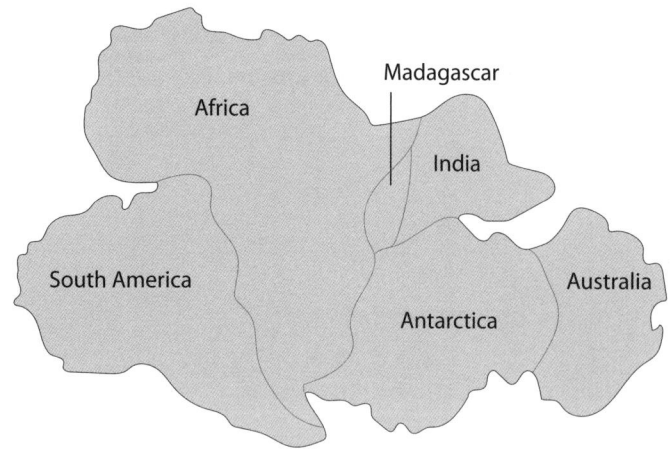

Describe what has happened to these continents in the last 200 million years to move them to their current positions.

....

....

3 Which statements are evidence for tectonic plates?

Tick (✓) all correct statements.

The same types of fossils have been found in different continents. ☐

Volcanoes and earthquakes are more likely to happen in particular places. ☐

There is more land north of the equator than south of the equator. ☐

The alignment of magnetic materials in rocks varies with the age of the rock. ☐

Each of the continents has parts that have different climates. ☐

Exercise 6.5B Tectonic plates

Practice

In this exercise, you will think about what tectonic plates are and how they move.

1 **a** List each of these parts of the Earth in order from hottest to coldest.

   mantle   **inner core**   **crust**   **outer core**

   ....

b One of these parts contains large convection currents.

   i State which part.

   ....

   ii Describe what causes these convection currents.

   ....

   ....

   ....

   iii Describe how these convection currents cause the movement of tectonic plates.

   ....

   ....

   ....

2   The diagram shows a feature called the mid-Atlantic ridge.

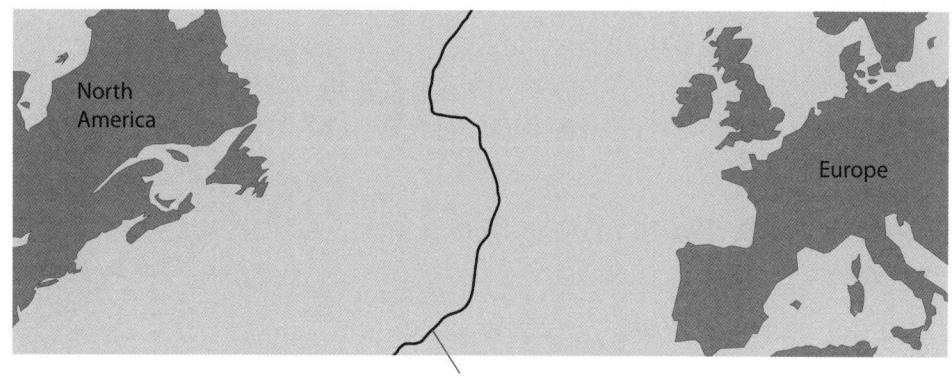

mid-Atlantic ridge

The mid-Atlantic ridge is a long area under the Atlantic Ocean where the Earth's crust is being pushed up by convection from below.

a   Use this information, and ideas about tectonic plates, to suggest why the continents of North America and Europe are moving away from each other.

    ....

    ....

    ....

    ....

b   Most of the underwater volcanoes and earthquakes in the Atlantic Ocean occur along the mid-Atlantic ridge. Suggest why.

    ....

    ....

    ....

    ....

Exercise 6.5C Evidence for tectonic plates

Challenge

In this exercise, you will consider the evidence for tectonic plates.

1 a Describe what is meant by tectonic plates.

....

....

b Briefly describe what causes the movement of tectonic plates.

....

....

....

....

2 a In the year 1912, a scientist called Alfred Wegener was the first person to suggest that the Earth's continents were slowly moving. Suggest why people did not believe this theory in 1912.

....

....

....

b A GPS system uses artificial satellites to accurately work out positions on Earth. GPS systems are commonly used in navigation applications.

Scientists have used GPS systems to show that the North American continent is moving towards the west at a speed of 23 mm per year.

i Explain how this provides evidence for tectonic plates.

....

....

    ii   Assuming that North America moves at a constant speed of 23 mm per year, calculate the time taken for this continent to move by 1 km.

.... years

3   Explain how each of these facts is evidence for tectonic plates.

    a   Scientists have found fossils of small mammals in South America that appear to be very similar to other fossils of the same age found in Africa.

....

....

....

    b   A magnetic material called magnetite is found in some rocks. The alignment of magnetite is always in the same direction as the Earth's magnetic field when the rock forms.
           The alignment of magnetite reverses in the rock moving away from the new rock, as shown in the diagram.

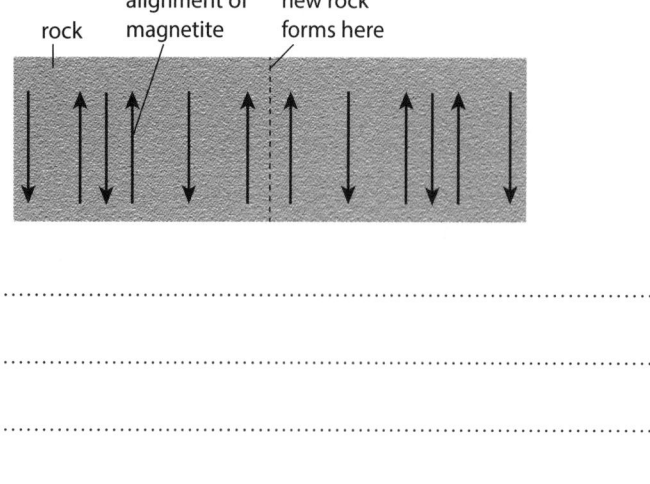

....

....

....

....

....

....

7 ▸ Genes and inheritance

▸ 7.1 Chromosomes, genes and DNA

Exercise 7.1 Chromosomes, genes and DNA

Focus

In this exercise, you will practise writing about chromosomes, genes and DNA.

The diagrams show a plant cell and an animal cell.

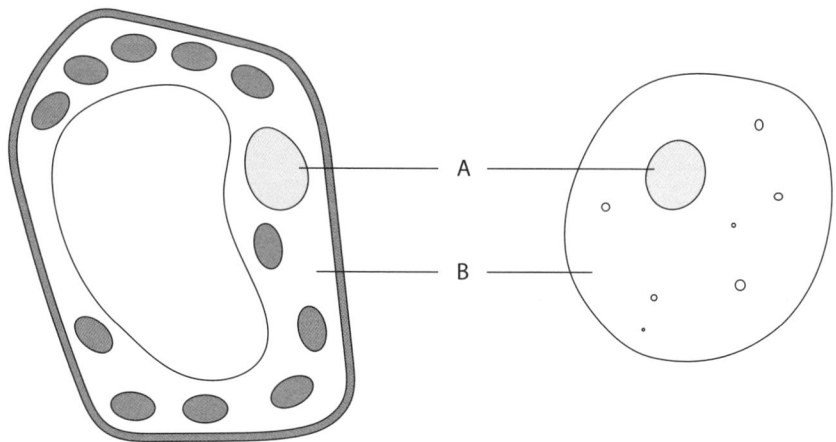

1   Name the parts labelled A and B.

   A ....   B ....

2   Write the letter X in **each** cell to show where the chromosomes are found.

Practice

3   Write a sentence, in your own words, using each of the words.
Try to include some scientific information in each sentence.

chromosome

....

....

gene

....

....

DNA

....

....

Challenge

4   When a plant or animal grows, or when it needs to repair damage
to its body, some of its cells divide to form two new cells.

Before this happens, all the DNA in the original cell is copied.
Each new cell then gets a complete copy of all the DNA in the
original cell.

Suggest why it is important that this happens.

....

....

....

....

> 7.2 Gametes and inheritance

Exercise 7.2 Egg cells and sperm cells

In this exercise, you will use information from a diagram to complete a comparison table about the structure of egg cells and sperm cells.

Focus

1   Complete these sentences about egg cells and sperm cells.

Choose from the list.

> cytoplasm   egg   female   fertilisation   gametes
> male   nucleus   sperm   swimming

Egg cells and sperm cells are specialised cells called ....

Egg cells are .... and sperm cells are ....

A sperm cell can join with an egg cell in a process called ....

All .... cells contain one X chromosome, but .... cells can contain an X chromosome or a Y chromosome.

Practice

The diagrams show an egg cell and a sperm cell.

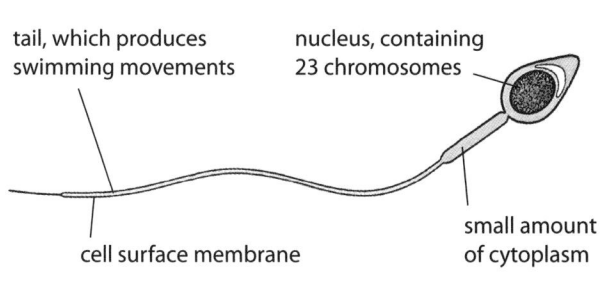
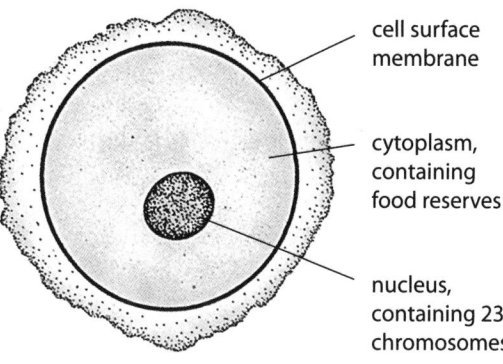

2   Complete the table to compare the structures of these two gametes.
    Use the labels on the diagrams to find information to write in the
    table. One comparison has been made for you.

    In the table:

    •   Write comparable points opposite each other.

    •   Draw a line underneath each pair of points.

    •   Include similarities, as well as differences.

Egg cell	Sperm cell
has food reserves in the cytoplasm	does not have food reserves in the cytoplasm

Challenge

3   Choose **two** of the differences you have described in the table.

    Explain how these differences help the sperm cell and the egg cell to
    carry out their functions.

    1st difference

    ....

    ....

    ....

    2nd difference

    ....

    ....

    ....

> 7.3 Variation

Exercise 7.3A Recording variation

Focus

In this exercise, you will practise completing a results table. Then you will use your results table to draw a bar chart.

Arun's class has a garden outside the classroom.

Arun's teacher gives him some canna lily tubers to plant in the garden. Tubers are parts of a plant that grow underground. They can be dug up and planted in the soil, where they will grow into complete new plants.

Arun and Marcus plant the tubers. Each tuber grows into a plant and produces flowers.

The boys count the number of lily plants with different-coloured flowers.

Here is the table that they make.

Flower colour	Yellow	White	Red	Orange
tally	|||||	|||	||||	||||| ||
number of plants				

1   Complete the last row of Arun and Marcus's results table.

2   Calculate the total number of lily plants.

....

3   Use Arun's and Marcus's results table to draw a bar chart.

Put **flower colour** on the horizontal axis.

Put **number of plants** on the vertical axis.

Use a pencil and ruler to draw your bar chart.

Leave spaces between the bars.

Do not shade the bars.

4   All canna lilies belong to the same species.

What word do we use to describe differences between individuals that belong to the same species?

Circle the correct answer.

    adaptations   features   frequency   variation

Exercise 7.3B Variation in holly leaves

Practice

This exercise gives you more practice in calculating a mean, and in recording variation in a results table and a frequency diagram. This time, you have to work out both the axis labels and scales yourself.

Sofia investigated variation in the number of prickles on holly leaves.
The photograph shows the leaves.

1   Count the number of prickles on each leaf, and write them down.

   ....

   ....

2   Calculate the mean number of prickles on a holly leaf. Show how you worked out your answer.

                    mean number of prickles ....

3 Draw a results table, and fill it in to show Sofia's results. Organise the results so that you can use them to draw a frequency diagram.

4 Draw a frequency diagram to show Sofia's results.

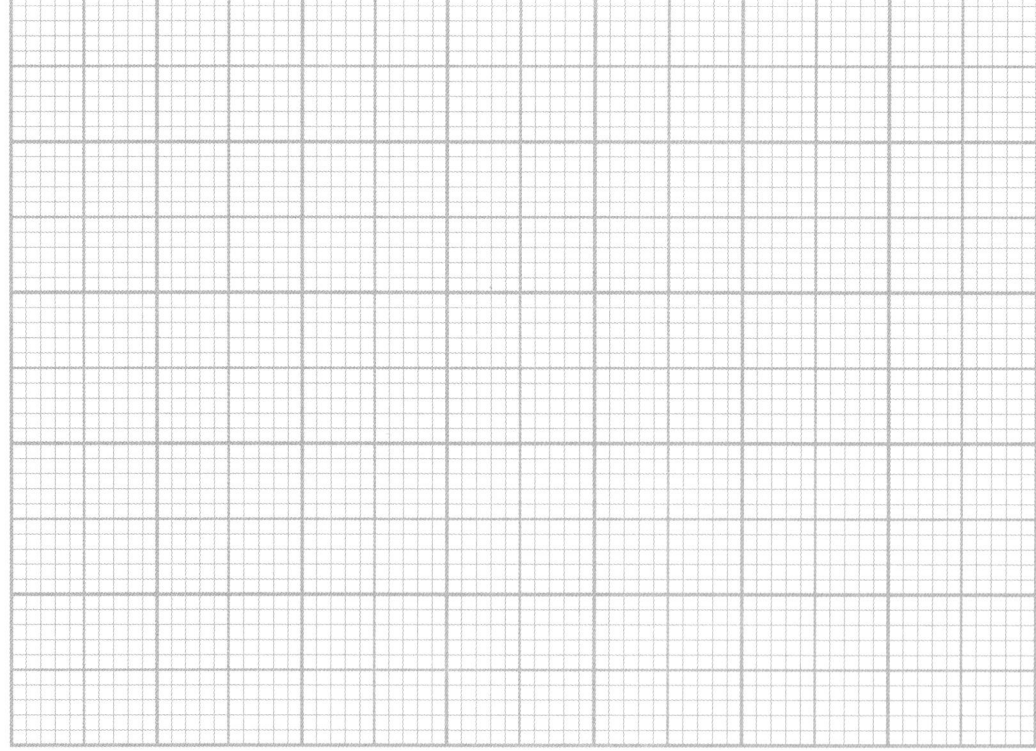

5 State one other feature that shows variation in these holly leaves.

....

Exercise 7.3C Variation in pea pods

Challenge

In this challenge task, you will choose a characteristic that shows variation in a plant species and decide how to record data about your chosen characteristic. You will then construct a frequency diagram.

The drawing shows 20 pea pods, opened to show the seeds inside.

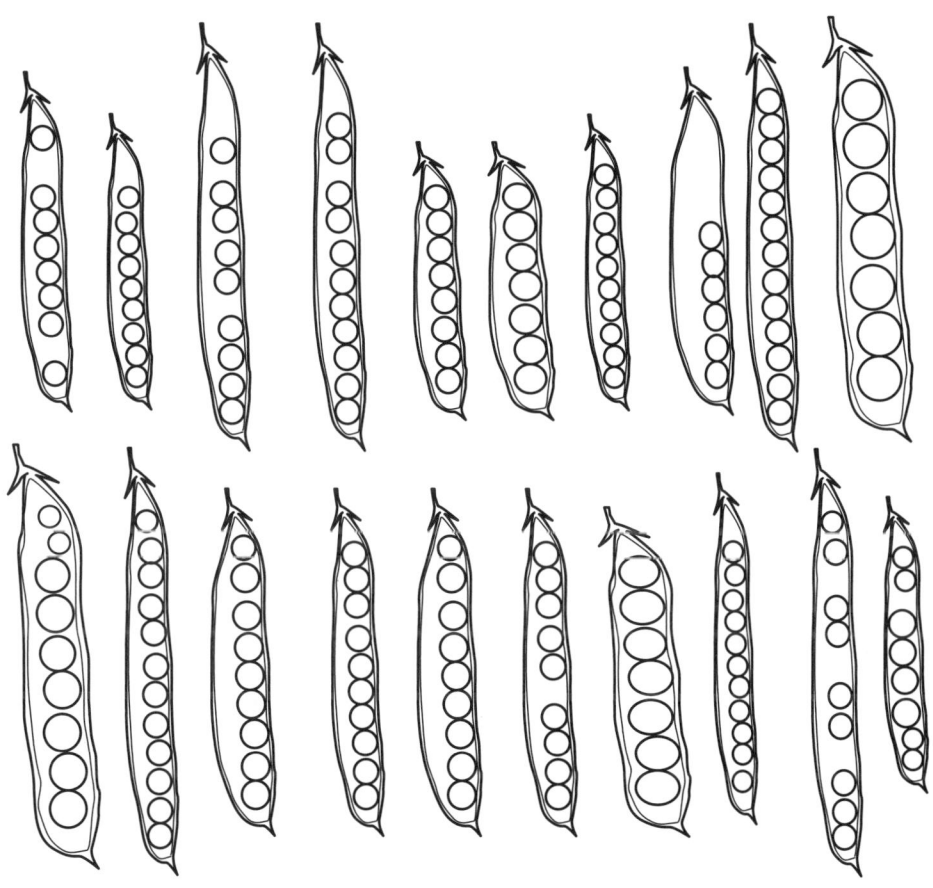

1   List **three** features that show variation in these pea pods.

....

....

....

2 Choose **one** of the features in your list that you can assess by counting it.

Chosen feature ....

Count this feature in each of the pea pods.
Write your results in the space below.

3 Decide on categories that you can group your results into.
Try to have at least four categories, but no more than ten.

4 Construct a tally chart in which you can record your results.

5   Use your results to construct a frequency diagram.

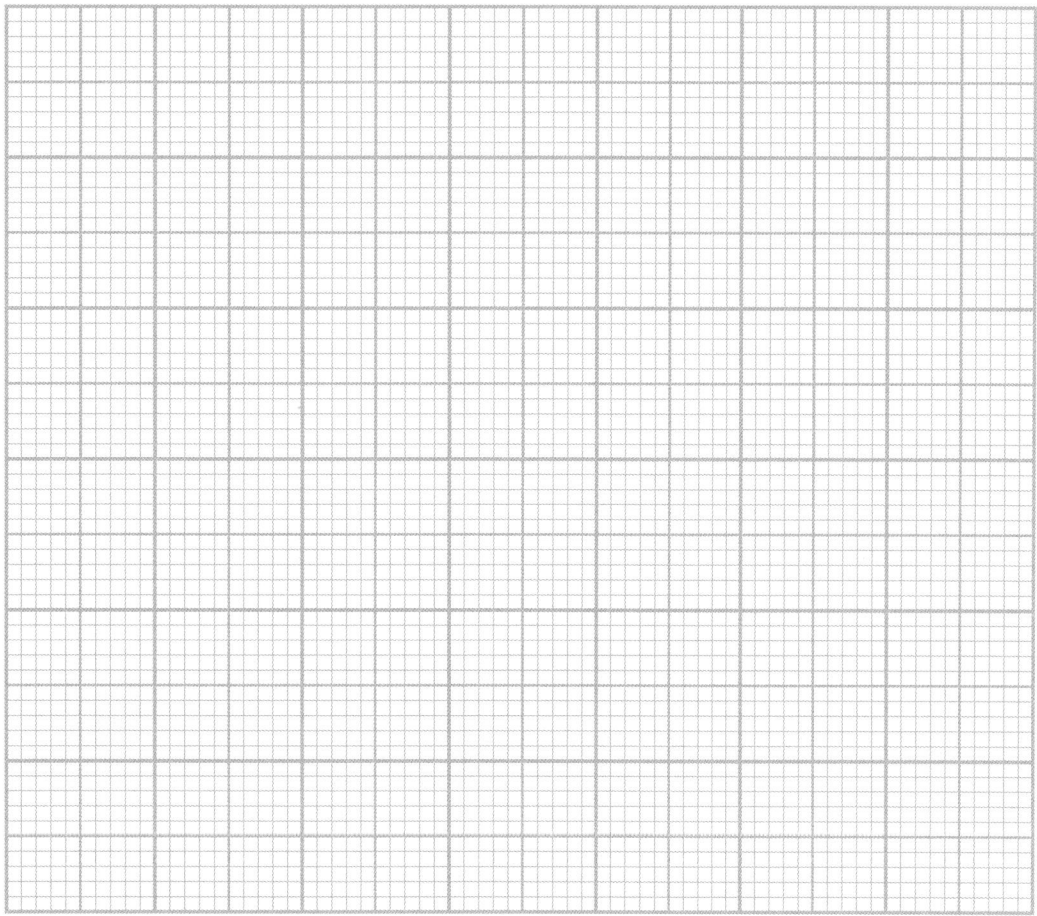

> 7.4 Natural selection

Exercise 7.4A Blue-tailed lizards

Focus

In this exercise, you will improve your understanding of how natural selection works.

When a lizard is attacked by a predator, the lizard's tail falls off.

The tail squirms violently, attracting the attention of the predator.

While the predator is attacking the tail, the lizard runs off and hides. It grows a new tail.

Some lizards have blue tails. Snakes are especially good at seeing the colour blue.

In places where snakes are the main predators of lizards, the lizards are more likely to have blue tails.

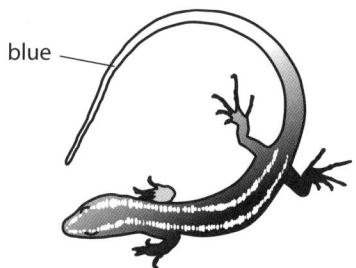

blue

1   The lizard's genes determine the colour of its tail.

Which part of the lizard's cells contains genes?

cell membrane ☐   cytoplasm ☐   nucleus ☐

2   Two parent lizards with blue tails pass on their genes for blue tails to their offspring.

What is the word we use to describe passing on genes from parents to offspring?

DNA ☐   inheritance ☐   variation ☐

3   A population of lizards lives on an island where there are no snakes. Some of the lizards have brown tails and some have blue tails.

Some snakes arrive on the island.

Explain why the lizards with brown tails are more likely to be eaten by snakes than the lizards with blue tails.

....

....

....

4   In the next generation, more lizards are born with blue tails than with brown tails.

Tick (✓) the correct explanation.

The lizards change their tail colour so that they will not be eaten by snakes. ☐

More parent lizards with blue tails survive, so they are the ones that reproduce. They pass on their genes for blue tails to their offspring. ☐

The lizards learn that it is safer to have a blue tail, so they have offspring with blue tails. ☐

Exercise 7.4B Camouflaged caterpillars

Practice

In this exercise, you will make sure that you understand how natural selection works. You also think about designing good experiments.

Sofia and Zara are looking at caterpillars.

They find out that a species of moth usually has green caterpillars, but sometimes has yellow caterpillars.

The girls have an idea that they decide to test:

> In a grassy area, green caterpillars are less likely to be found by a predator than yellow caterpillars.

Sofia and Zara use pieces of spiral-shaped pasta to represent caterpillars. They make 100 'caterpillars'.

They colour 50 of the 'caterpillars' green, and 50 yellow.

They put all the coloured pasta pieces together in a bucket and shake them up. The girls then spread the pasta pieces over a grassy area outside the classroom. Then they ask Marcus to pick up the first 20 pasta caterpillars he can find.

1   What measurements or observations should the girls make to test their idea? Tick (✓) the correct answer.

the time taken for Marcus to find 20 caterpillars ☐

how many green caterpillars and how many yellow caterpillars Marcus picks up ☐

which hand Marcus uses to pick up the caterpillars ☐

2   The girls decide that they need more results, so that they can make a reliable conclusion.

What should they do next?

Tick (✓) the correct answer.

Repeat the experiment five times with the same caterpillars, using five different students to collect them. ☐

Repeat the experiment using 25 green caterpillars and 75 yellow caterpillars. ☐

Repeat the experiment using 50 blue caterpillars and 50 red caterpillars. ☐

3   Sofia and Zara think about why the real caterpillars of the moth are more likely to be green than yellow, when living in a grassy area.

They write five sentences to explain how natural selection could make this happen. Their sentences are here but in the wrong order.

Write a number next to each sentence to show the correct order. The first number has been written for you.

A   The adult moths mate and lay fertilised eggs. ☐

B   So adult moths are more likely to contain genes for producing green caterpillars than for producing yellow caterpillars. ☐

C   So more green caterpillars hatch out of the eggs than yellow caterpillars. ☐

D   Green caterpillars are more likely to survive and grow up into adult moths. ☐ 1

E   The fertilised eggs are more likely to contain genes for producing green caterpillars than for producing yellow caterpillars. ☐

Exercise 7.4C Woolly mammoths

Challenge

In this exercise, you will practise using the ideas of natural selection to suggest an explanation for how a species of animal developed. You will need to write your ideas down on rough paper first. Try to put plenty of detail into your answer and use scientific terms where you can.

Woolly mammoths lived in northern Europe, North America and Siberia. The last woolly mammoth is thought to have died about 4000 years ago.

Woolly mammoths had very long, thick hair, which insulated them in the cold climates in which they lived. They also had huge tusks. Scientists think that they may have used their tusks to clear away snow, to find plants underneath that they could eat.

Woolly mammoths are thought to have developed from steppe mammoths. Steppe mammoths looked rather like elephants. They had less fur and shorter tusks than woolly mammoths. Woolly mammoths probably developed from steppe mammoths when the climate got much colder, during one of the Ice Ages.

Use the ideas of natural selection to suggest how woolly mammoths may have developed from steppe mammoths.

....

....

....

....

....

....

....

....

....

....

....

....

....

....

....

....

....

....

....

....

....

....

....

....

....

8 Rates of reaction

> 8.1 Measuring rates of reaction

Exercise 8.1A Showing the change in rate of reaction on a graph

Focus

This exercise will give you some practice at interpreting a graph showing the rate of reaction.

Magnesium ribbon is added to hydrochloric acid.

The gas hydrogen is given off. This is collected and its volume measured in a syringe.

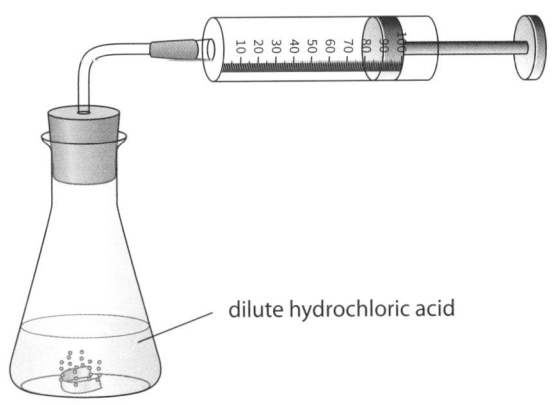

dilute hydrochloric acid

This graph shows the volume of gas collected as time progresses. It shows the rate of reaction between magnesium ribbon and hydrochloric acid.

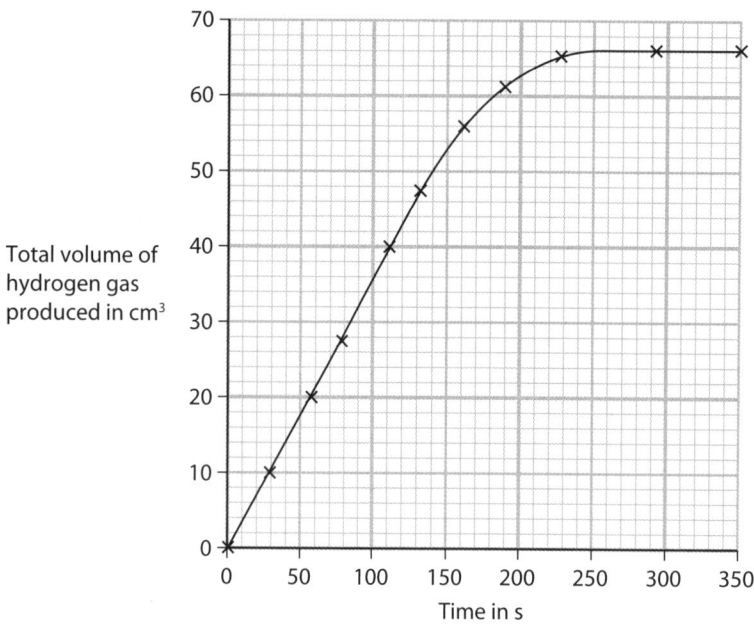

Remember the slope of the line on the graph tells you the rate of reaction. The steeper the line, the faster the reaction.

1   Tick (✓) the correct answer.

The greatest rate of reaction is:

between 0 seconds and 100 seconds   ☐

between 150 seconds and 250 seconds   ☐

between 250 seconds and 350 seconds.   ☐

2   Tick (✓) the correct answer.

The lowest rate of reaction is:

between 0 seconds and 100 seconds   ☐

between 150 seconds and 250 seconds   ☐

between 250 seconds and 350 seconds.   ☐

3   How much hydrogen is produced between 0 seconds and 100 seconds?

....

4   Calculate how much hydrogen gas is produced between 150 seconds and 250 seconds.

....

Exercise 8.1B Changes in the rate of reaction

Practice

This exercise will help you to interpret data and plot a graph.

Sofia investigated the rate of reaction between magnesium metal and hydrochloric acid.

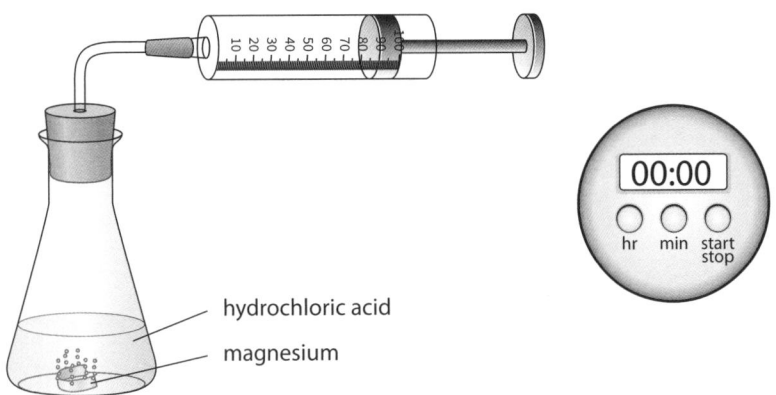

1   Write the word equation for this reaction.

    ....

2   Sofia repeated her experiment three times. Explain why she did this.

    ....

    ....

    ....

3   The table contains her results. Complete the table.

Time in s	Volume of gas collected in cm^3			
	Attempt 1	Attempt 2	Attempt 3	Mean
0	0	0	0	
20	28	31	31	
40	39	48	42	
60	56	53	57	
80	60	59	61	
100	60	59	61	

4   Plot a graph of Sofia's results. Draw a line of best fit.

Volume of gas
collected in cm³

Time in s

5   When did the reaction end? Explain how you know this.

....

....

6   Complete the following sentence.

The reaction is fastest between .... seconds

and .... seconds.

Exercise 8.1C Explaining observations

Challenge

In this exercise, you will plot a graph and explain the reasons for the changes in the rate of reaction.

Marcus wanted to investigate the rate of reaction between magnesium ribbon and hydrochloric acid. He collected hydrogen gas and measured its volume every 30 seconds.

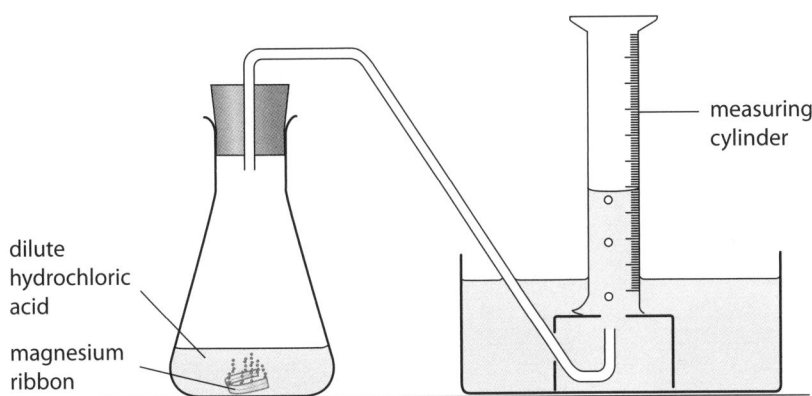

1   Write the symbol equation for this reaction.

....

2   Look carefully at the equipment and suggest any sources of error that Marcus is likely to have. Suggest how he could try to overcome these.

....

....

....

....

Marcus's results are shown in this table.

Time in s	0	30	60	90	120	150	180	210	240	270	300	330	360
Total volume of hydrogen collected in cm^3	0	10	18	26	29	33	36	38	39	41	41	41	41

3 Use these results to plot a graph.

4   Describe what your graph shows.

     ....

     ....

     ....

     ....

5   Calculate the average rate of reaction between 30 and 60 seconds.

     ....

     ....

6   Calculate the average rate of reaction between 150 and 180 seconds.

     ....

     ....

7   Explain using collision theory, why the graph is the shape it is.

     ....

     ....

     ....

     ....

     ....

     ....

> 8.2 Surface area and the rate of reaction

Exercise 8.2 Surface area and the rate of reaction

Focus

This exercise will help you to interpret graphs about surface area and the rate of reaction and to consider some practical aspects of the investigation.

Zara investigated the effect of surface area on the rate of reaction. She used a flat piece of zinc and a lump of zinc of the same mass. She placed each of them in hydrochloric acid and carried out the reaction, collecting the gas over water in a measuring cylinder.

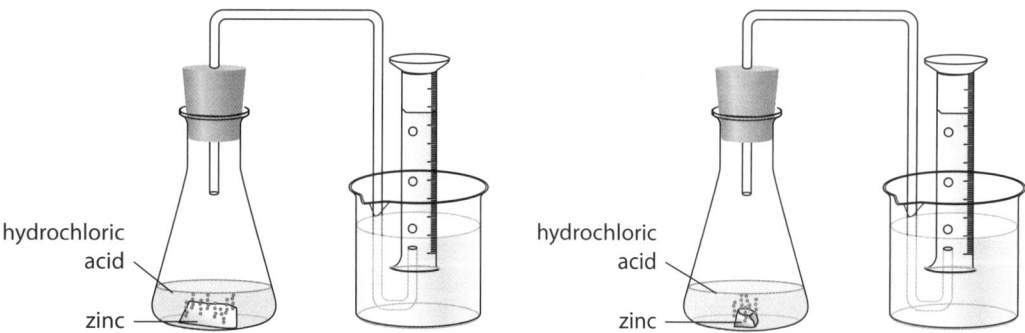

1   Which gas is being collected over water?

....

2   Write the word equation for this reaction.

3 What practical problems might Zara have in obtaining her results,
if she uses this method of collecting the gas?

....

....

....

Zara plotted her results of the investigation on the same graph.

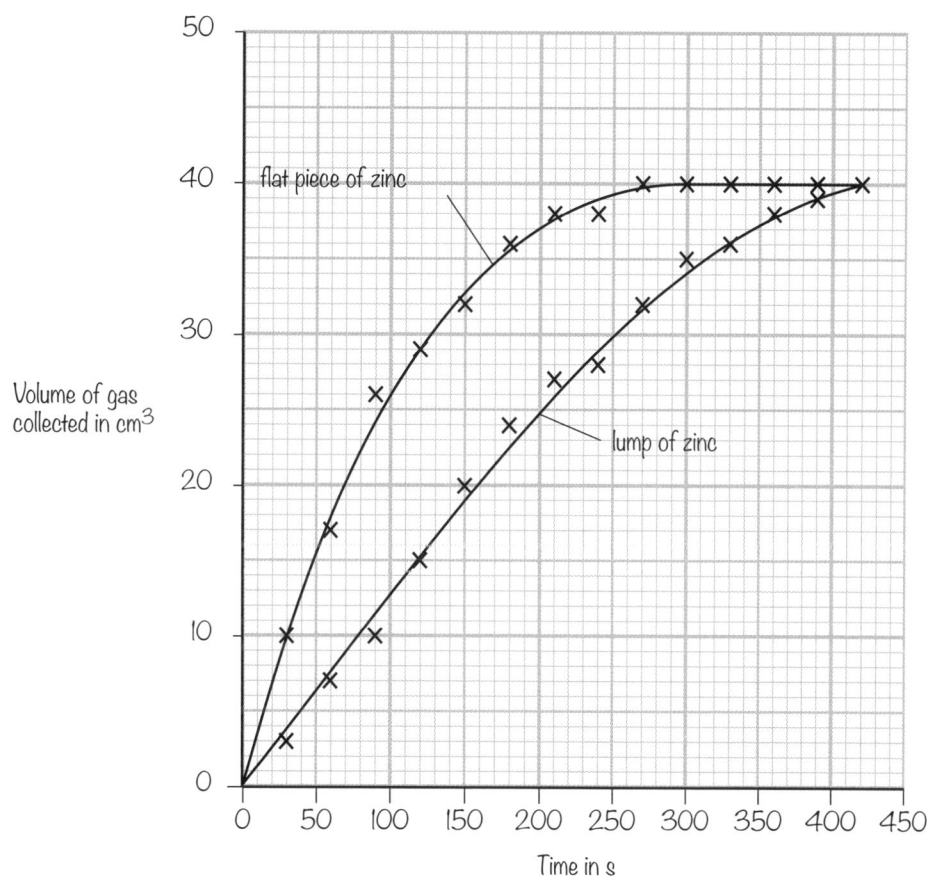

4 Circle the phrase that correctly completes the sentence.

The total volume of gas produced in the two reactions after
420 seconds was:

- higher in the one with the lump of zinc

- lower in the one with the lump of zinc

- the same.

Practice

5   Describe the graph for the reaction with the flat piece of zinc.
    Remember to include the times at which the reaction was fastest
    and slowest.

    ....

    ....

    ....

    ....

    ....

    ....

6   How is the line of best fit for the reaction using the piece of zinc
    different from the one using the lump of zinc.

    ....

    ....

    ....

    ....

Challenge

7   Explain using collision theory the difference you have described in
    question 6.

    ....

    ....

    ....

    ....

8   On the graph, draw the line you would expect to see if Zara did the
    experiment again using the same mass of powdered zinc.

9   Explain, using collision theory, why you have drawn the graph this shape.

....

....

....

....

....

....

> 8.3 Temperature and the rate of reaction

Exercise 8.3A Explaining changes in the rate of reaction

Focus

In this exercise, you will use particle theory to explain changes in the rate of reaction.

For a reaction to take place, particles of the reactants must collide with enough energy to react with each other.

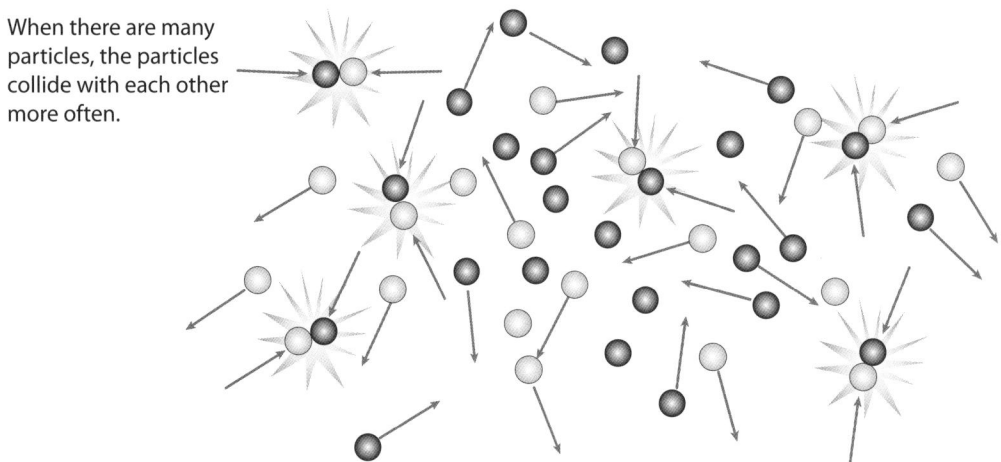

When there are many particles, the particles collide with each other more often.

1   Explain the following, using particle theory and ideas about collisions.

   a   The rate of reaction at the start of a reaction is high.

   ....

   ....

   ....

   b   The rate of reaction decreases after a time.

   ....

   ....

   ....

2   When particles have more energy, they move more quickly.

   Explain, using the same ideas, why increasing the temperature increases the rate of reaction.

   ....

   ....

   ....

Exercise 8.3B Temperature and the rate of reaction

Practice

This exercise will help you to plan investigations.

1   Sofia and Marcus are investigating the effect of temperature on the rate of reaction.

    •   They have been told that they can use a suitable metal (but not in powdered form) and an acid.

    •   They will use the temperature range 20 °C to 70 °C with an interval of 10 °C.

    •   They will start the stopwatch as soon as the metal is placed in the acid and stop it again when the reaction stops.

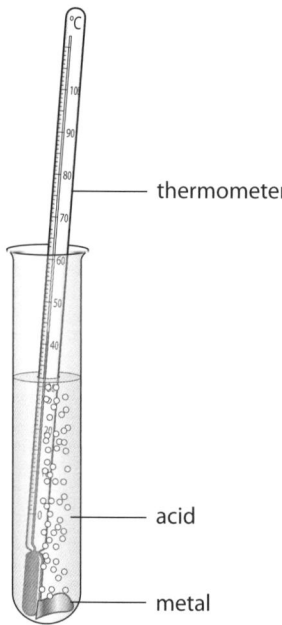

    thermometer

    acid

    metal

a   Suggest a suitable metal and acid to use in this investigation.

....

....

b What safety precautions should Sofia and Marcus take?

....

....

....

c Which variables must they keep the same in this investigation to ensure that the test is fair?

....

....

....

....

d How will they know when the reaction has stopped?

....

....

e Construct a results table for their investigation. You cannot fill in their results – just leave that part of the table blank.

Challenge

In this exercise, you will suggest the trend in the results of an investigation and explain the reasons for the changes in the rate of reaction of an acid and a metal. Read through the practice exercise before you attempt these questions.

2 **a** On the grid below, sketch the graph you would expect Sofia and Marcus's results to produce.

Time for reaction to take place in s

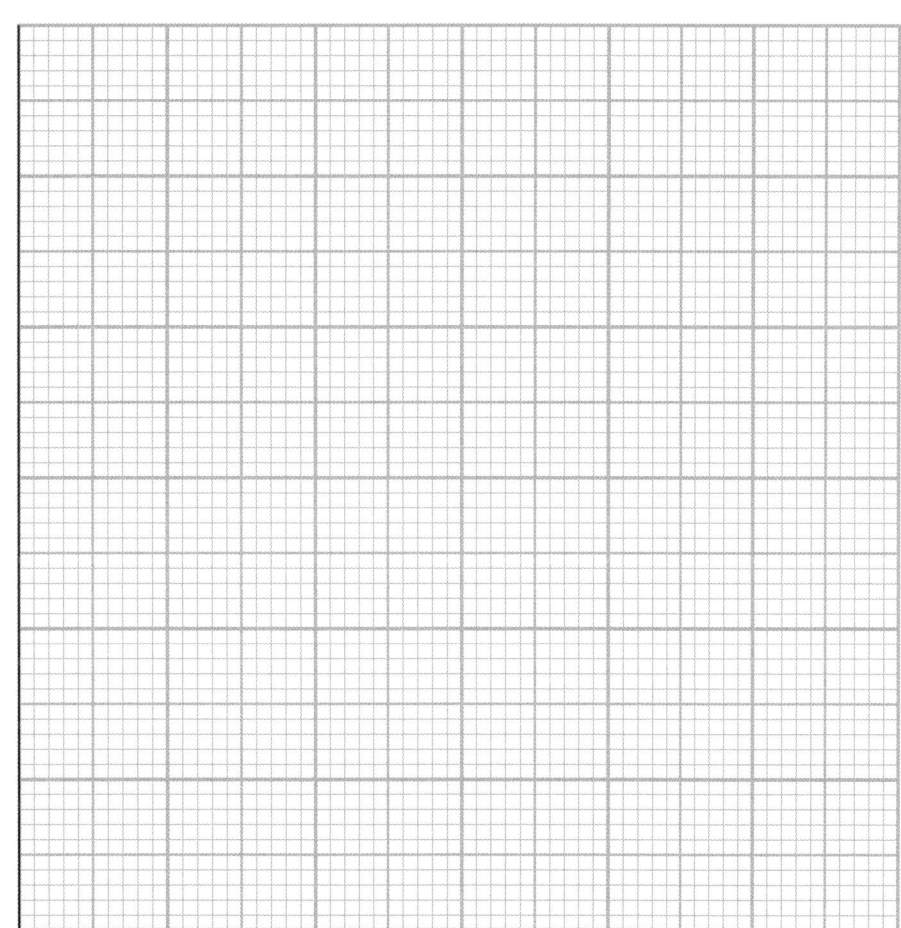

Temperature in °C

b Use particle theory to explain in detail why a change in temperature changes the rate of reaction.

....

....

....

....

....

....

c If Sofia and Marcus repeated their investigation using the same mass of metal but in powdered form, how would the graph be different? Add your idea to the graph in part **a** and label the line clearly. Explain the reasons for these results.

....

....

> 8.4 Concentration and the rate of reaction

Exercise 8.4A Concentration and the rate of reaction

Focus

This exercise will help you to plan investigations and explain the reasons for changes in the rate of reaction.

Zara and Sofia are investigating the effect of changing the concentration on the rate of reaction between dilute sulfuric acid and zinc. They have been given a number of pieces of zinc of the same size and mass but only one bottle of dilute sulfuric acid. Their first task is to make up five different concentrations of the acid.

1   Explain how they would make solutions of five different concentrations of sulfuric acid. Remember to explain how they will measure the liquids accurately.

    ....

    ....

    ....

    ....

    ....

    ....

Zara and Sofia carry out their investigation. They keep the volume of acid used the same each time. The mass and size of the zinc used is the same each time. The temperature of the acid is the same each time.

2   What do the girls measure when they carry out the reaction?

    ....

3 List the equipment they will need to carry out this investigation.

....

....

....

....

....

4 What would you expect them to find out in this investigation?

....

....

....

5 Explain why you think they will get these results.
You may use diagrams if it helps you to explain.

....

....

....

....

Exercise 8.4B Which results are which?

Practice

In this exercise, you will identify sets of results and describe, compare and explain the results.

Arun carried out an investigation of the rate of reaction between magnesium and sulfuric acid, using different concentrations of acid.

The concentrations he used are shown in the table. The hydrogen gas produced was collected and its volume measured every 30 seconds.

Concentration	Volume of acid used in cm^3	Volume of water used in cm^3
×5	50	0
×4	40	10
×3	30	20
×2	20	30
×1	10	40
×0	0	50

1   The acid concentration ×0 was not used in this investigation. Why?

    ....

    ....

    ....

2   The graph below shows Arun's results for ×4 concentration,
    ×3 concentration and ×2 concentration.

    Arun has not labelled the concentrations on the graph.
    Label each line with the appropriate concentration.

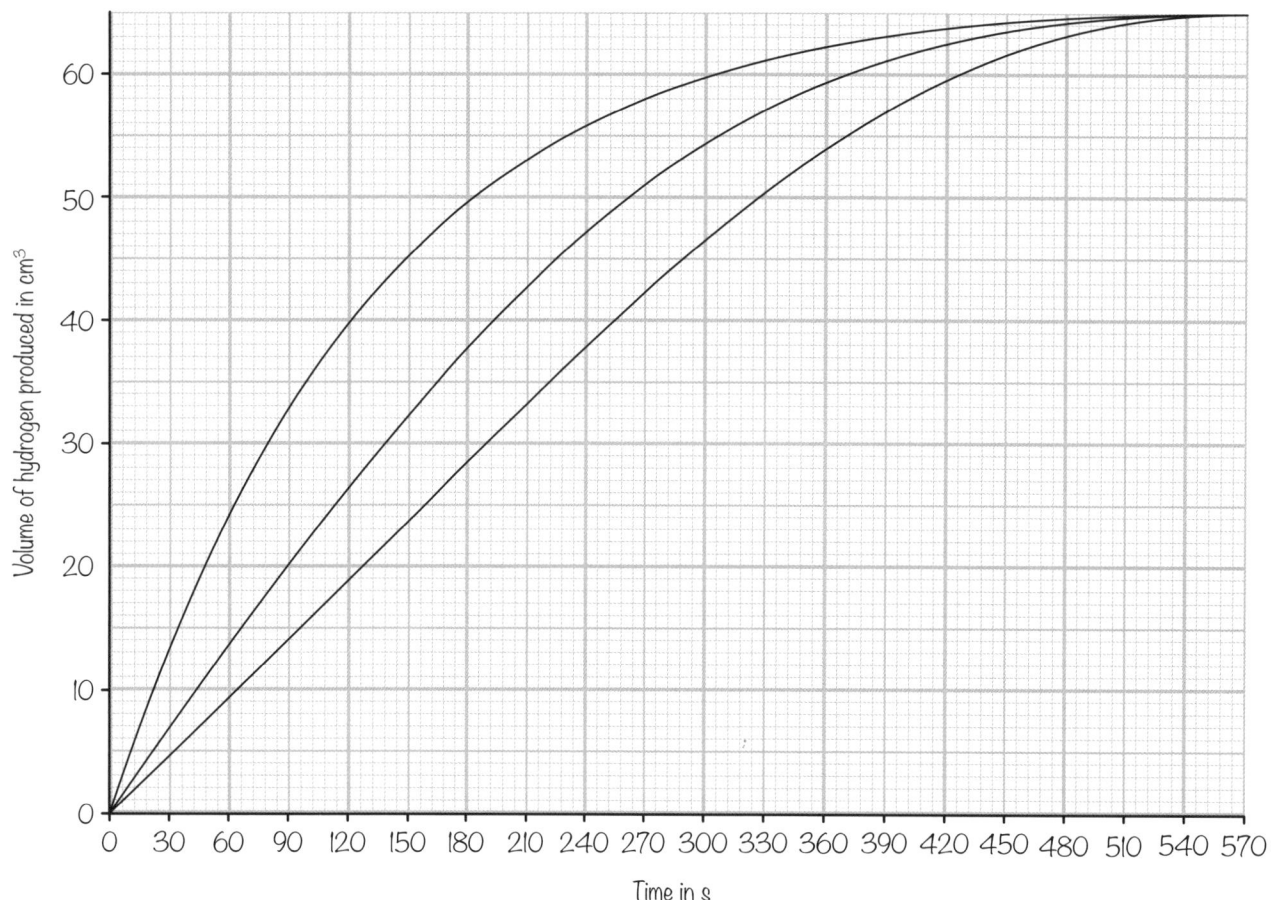

3   Compare the three sets of results and explain what they show.

    ....

    ....

    ....

    ....

    ....

    ....

4 Explain the three sets of results shown on the graph using particle and collision theory.

....

....

....

....

....

....

5 Sketch on the graph your predicted line for the ×5 concentration. Label the line.

Exercise 8.4C As fast as possible

Challenge

In this exercise, you will plan an experiment and explain the reasons for your decisions.

Marcus and Zara have been asked to carry out the reactions between marble chips and dilute acid and to collect $100\,cm^3$ of carbon dioxide in the shortest possible time.

They may use only $20\,g$ of marble chips and $50\,cm^3$ of standard dilute hydrochloric acid. They have access to a range of laboratory equipment.

1 Draw and label a diagram to show how they could carry out this reaction and collect the gas.

2 List all other equipment **not** shown in the diagram that they will need to use.

....

....

....

3 Which variables are the learners **not** permitted to change?

....

....

4 Which **two** variables could they change to give a faster rate of reaction?

Variable 1: ....

Variable 2: ....

5 Explain, for each of the variables you have stated in question 4, how changing it will increase the rate of reaction.

Variable 1:

....

....

....

....

....

Variable 2:

....

....

....

....

....

6   Describe how Marcus and Zara should carry out this experiment.

....

....

....

....

....

....

....

....

....

7   Suggest any practical difficulties in carrying out this experiment
     that may make the collection time longer than it should be.

....

....

....

....

....

....

....

....

....

9 ▶ Electricity

> 9.1 Parallel circuits

Exercise 9.1A Current flow in parallel circuits

Focus

In this exercise, you will describe how current flows in a parallel circuit.

1   The circuit diagram shows two lamps connected to a cell.

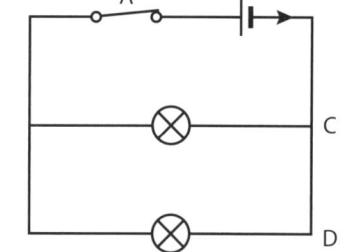

    a   Explain whether this a series or a parallel circuit.

       ....

       ....

    b   Current flows in the direction shown by the arrow.
       At which point in the circuit does current divide?
       Write the letter: ....

2   The circuit diagram opposite shows the current at two positions.
    Calculate the current at position X in the circuit.
    Show your working.

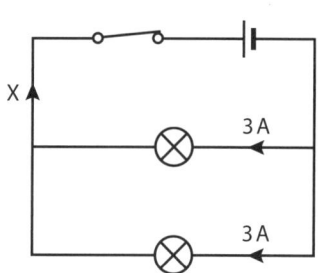

                                               ....A

3   This circuit contains two identical buzzers. The current at one position in the circuit is shown.

Calculate the currents at positions P and R in the circuit.

Show your working.

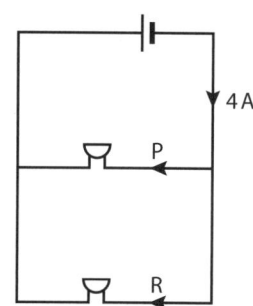

P = ... A

R = ... A

Exercise 9.1B Facts about parallel circuits

Practice

In this exercise, you will describe parallel circuits.

1   Which of these are correct facts about parallel circuits.

Tick (✓) all that apply:

There is more than one path for current to flow in a parallel circuit. ☐

There are no branches in a parallel circuit. ☐

Current divides through different parts of a parallel circuit. ☐

When one component fails in a parallel circuit, all components stop working. ☐

2   The diagram shows a parallel circuit.

The circuit has two identical lamps and four ammeters.

a   Which ammeter will show the same current as A_1?

     ....

b   Which ammeter will show the same current as A_2?

     ....

c   Which ammeter will show half the current shown on A_4?

     ....

d   Which ammeter will show double the current shown on A_3?

     ....

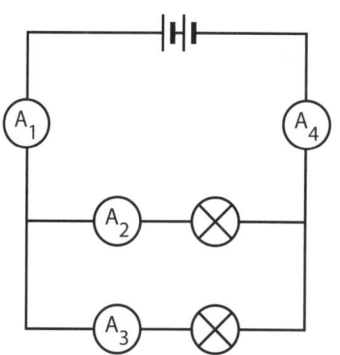

3   This circuit has three identical lamps and four ammeters.

Which facts about this circuit are true?

Tick (✓) **two** boxes.

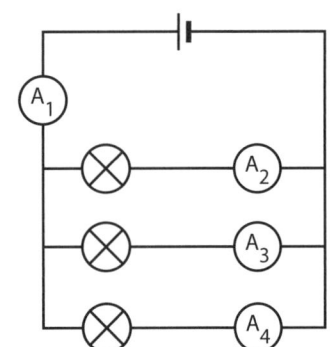

The reading on A_1 must be the largest of all four ammeters.   ☐

The reading on A_2 must be smaller than that on A_1.   ☐

The reading on A_4 must be smaller than that on A_3.   ☐

The readings on A_1, A_2 and A_3 must be the same.   ☐

The readings on all four ammeters must be the same.   ☐

Exercise 9.1C Understanding current in parallel circuits

Challenge

In this exercise, you will show your understanding of current in parallel circuits.

This circuit has two identical lamps, a buzzer and four ammeters.

Questions 1 and 2 refer to this circuit.

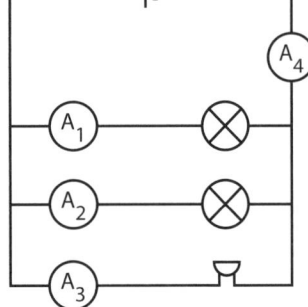

1   The reading on ammeter A_3 shows the smallest current in the circuit.

a   Describe how the readings on ammeters A_1, A_2 and A_3 compare.

....

....

....

....

b   Write an equation to calculate the reading on A_4, using the readings on A_1, A_2 and A_3.

....

2 The buzzer in the circuit stops working. Ammeter A_3 now reads zero. State the effect of this change on:

a the readings on ammeters A_1 and A_2

....

b the reading on ammeter A_4.

....

> 9.2 Current and voltage in parallel circuits

Exercise 9.2A Voltage

Focus

In this exercise, you will think about voltage and how to measure voltage.

1 a Write down the word for the unit of voltage.

....

b Batteries are made to have different voltages.

What does the voltage of a battery show?

Tick (✓) **one** box.

The current from the battery.　　　　　☐

The energy that the battery can supply.　☐

The length and width of the battery.　　☐

2 This circuit has a lamp and a buzzer in parallel. The voltage of the cell is shown.

a Write down the voltage across the lamp.

....

b Write down the voltage across the buzzer.

....

c   Name the component that is used to measure voltage.

....

3   This circuit has two identical lamps, L_1 and L_2.
The voltage of the battery is shown.

Which row in the table shows the voltage across lamp L_1
and lamp L_2?

Tick (✓) **one** row.

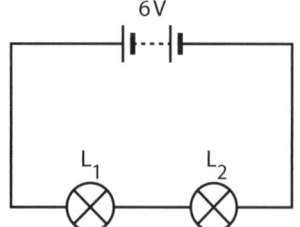

voltage across L_1 in V	voltage across L_2 in V	
3	3	☐
3	6	☐
6	3	☐
6	6	☐

Exercise 9.2B Current and voltage

Practice

In this exercise, you will think of current and voltage in circuits and
how to measure them.

1   This circuit has two lamps and a buzzer.

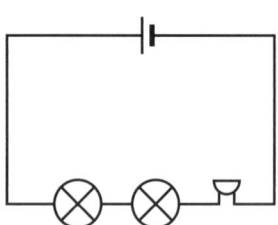

a   Copy the circuit diagram and add components that will
measure the current in the circuit, and will measure the
voltage across the buzzer at the same time.

b Describe how the voltages across the each of the lamps and across the buzzer are related to the voltage across the cell in this circuit.

....

....

c Another lamp is added in series.

State how this change affects:

i the current in the circuit

....

ii the voltage across the buzzer.

....

2 Arun builds the circuit shown in the drawing.

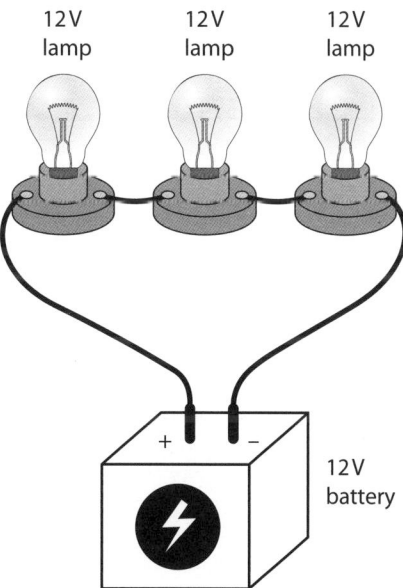

Each of the lamps is identical and rated at 12 V.
Arun uses a12 V battery.

a Explain why the lamps will **not** operate correctly in this circuit.

....

....

....

b   In the space below, draw a circuit diagram to show how Arun should connect three 12 V lamps to a 12 V battery so the lamps work properly.

Use standard circuit symbols in your diagram.

Exercise 9.2C Changes in current and voltage

Challenge

In this exercise, you will think about how adding components affects current and voltage.

1   A lamp, L_1, is connected to a cell as shown in this circuit.

State what will happen when each of these changes is made.

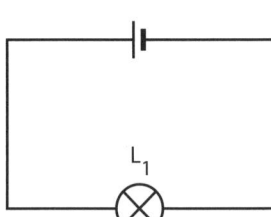

a   Another identical lamp is added in series with L_1.

i   The current in the circuit will ....

ii   The voltage across L_1 will ....

b   In this part of the question, explain your answers.

Another identical lamp is added in parallel with L_1.

i   The current through the cell will ....

because ....

....

   ii   The voltage across L_1 will ....

      because ....

      ....

2 Look at what each of these letters represents.

V_L = voltage across one lamp

N = number of identical lamps

V_C = voltage of the cell in the circuit

  a Which equation is correct for identical lamps connected in series?

    Tick (✓) **one** box.

    $V_L = \dfrac{N}{V_C}$ ☐

    $V_L = \dfrac{V_C}{N}$ ☐

    $V_L = V_C \times N$ ☐

    $V_L = V_C$ ☐

  b Which equation is correct for identical lamps connected one by one in parallel?

    Tick (✓) **one** box.

    $V_L = \dfrac{N}{V_C}$ ☐

    $V_L = \dfrac{V_C}{N}$ ☐

    $V_L = V_C \times N$ ☐

    $V_L = V_C$ ☐

› 9.3 Resistance

Exercise 9.3A Describing resistance

Focus

In this exercise, you will think about what resistance is.

1 Which of these is the unit of resistance?

Tick (✓) **one** box.

amps ☐

volts ☐

ohms ☐

joules ☐

2 In the space below, draw the circuit symbol for a resistor.

3 State what happens to the current in a circuit when the resistance in the circuit increases.

....

4 The voltage across a resistor is 12 V and the current through the resistor is 4A.

Calculate the resistance of the resistor.

Use the equation

$$resistance = \frac{voltage}{current}$$

Show your working.

.........................Ω

Exercise 9.3B Calculating resistance, voltage and current

Practice

In this exercise, you will calculate values of resistance, voltage and current.

1   Write the equation that relates resistance to voltage and current.

resistance =
....

2   Calculate the value of the resistor in each of these. Only part of each circuit is shown.

Show your working and give the unit with your answer.

a

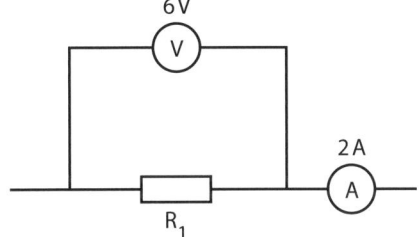

resistance of R_1 = ...

b

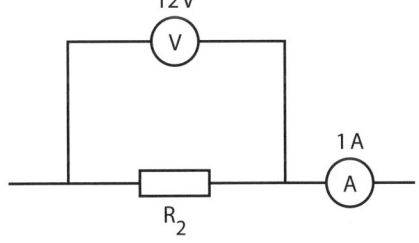

resistance of R_2 = ...

c

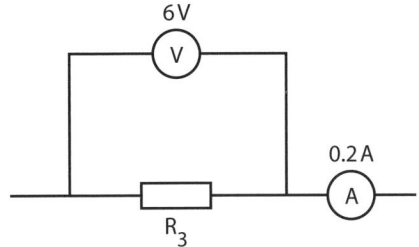

resistance of R_3 = ...

3   Calculate the reading on the voltmeter in each of these. Only part of each circuit is shown.

Show your working and give the unit with your answer.

a

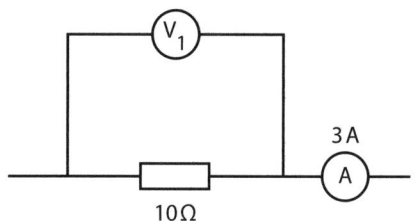

reading on V_1 = ...

b

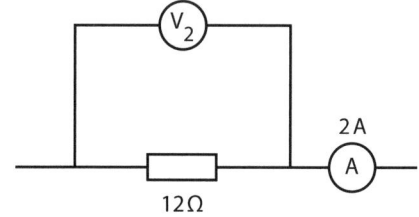

reading on V_2 = ...

c

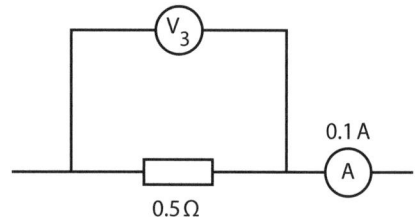

reading on V_3 = ...

4 Calculate the reading on the ammeter in each of these. Only part of each circuit is shown.

Show your working and give the unit with your answer.

a

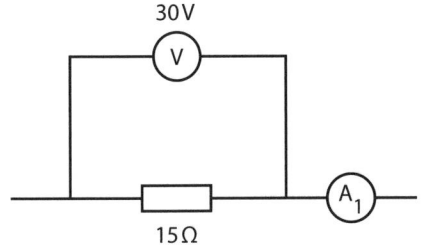

reading on A_1 = ...

b

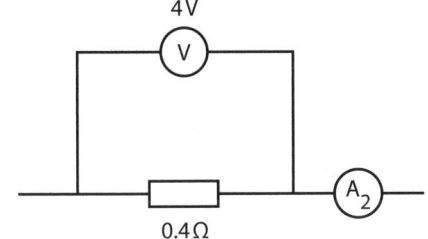

reading on A_2 = ...

c

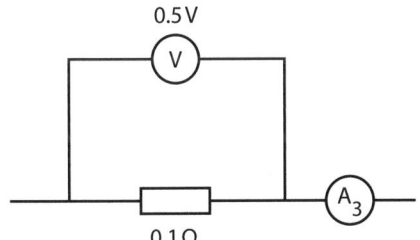

reading on A_3 = ...

Exercise 9.3C Ohm's law

Challenge

In this exercise, you will use information about Ohm's law to think about resistance.

1   Ohm's law relates resistance, voltage and current.

The equation for Ohm's law is

$$V = IR$$

a   State what the letter I represents in this equation.

   ....

b   Use the equation for Ohm's law to complete these sentences.

   As R increases and I stays the same, V ....

   As R increases and V stays the same, I ....

2   A resistor is connected in series with a cell. The current through the resistor is A amps. There are **no** other components.

Another identical resistor is added in series.

a   State the current through the resistors when the second resistor is added.

   ....

b   Explain your answer.

   ....

   ....

3   A piece of copper wire in a circuit is 25 cm long.

Which of these is most likely to be the resistance of this copper wire?

Tick (✓) **one** box.

   0.001 Ω   ☐

   10 Ω   ☐

   1000 Ω   ☐

   100 000 Ω   ☐

> 9.4 Practical circuits

Exercise 9.4A Variable resistors

Focus

In this exercise, you will describe variable resistors.

1 Draw the circuit symbol for a variable resistor.

2 Which of these could describe the resistance of a variable resistor?

Tick (✓) **one** box.

50 V only ☐

50 A only ☐

1–50 V ☐

1–50 Ω ☐

3 A variable resistor is connected in series with a lamp.

The resistance of the variable resistor is increased.

a State the effect on the current through the lamp.

....

b State the effect on the brightness of the lamp.

....

Exercise 9.4B Uses of variable resistors

Practice

In this exercise, you will describe some of the uses of variable resistors.

1 Describe the difference between a variable resistor and a fixed resistor.

....

....

2 Draw a circuit diagram to show how a variable resistor can be used to change the brightness of a lamp.

3 Draw a circuit diagram to show how one variable resistor can be used to change the brightness of two lamps that are connected in series.

4 Draw a circuit diagram to show how one variable resistor can be used to change the brightness of two lamps that are connected in parallel.

Exercise 9.4C Comparing circuits

Challenge

In this exercise, you will compare different circuit diagrams.

Use the circuit diagrams A–D to answer the questions in this exercise.

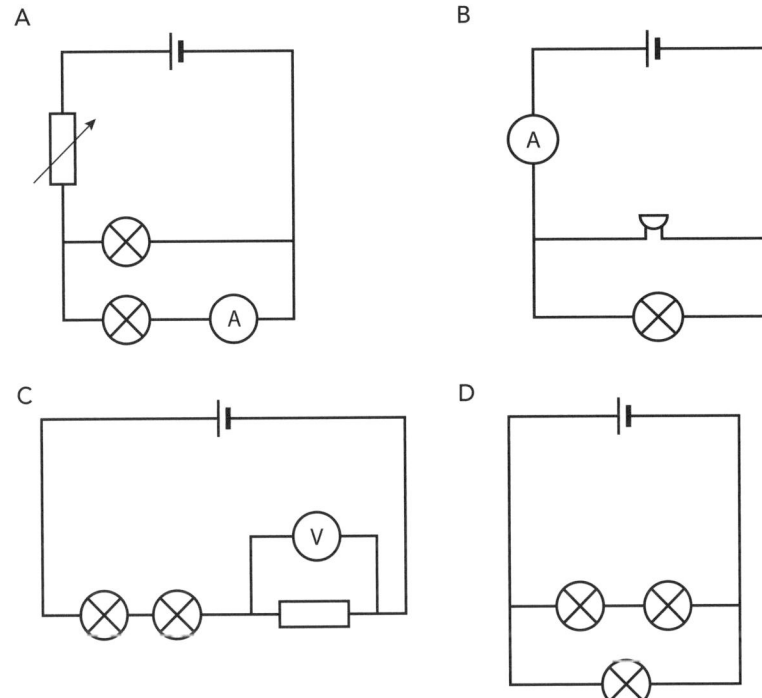

All the lamps in circuits A–D are identical.

The letters A–D can be used once, more than once or not at all.

1 Which circuit will show the voltage across one component?

Write the letter: ....

2 Which circuit will show the current through the cell?

Write the letter: ....

3 Which circuit contains lamps of different brightness?

Write the letter: ....

4 Which circuit will show the total current that flows through two components?

Write the letter: ....

5 Which circuits contain two lamps that have the same current?

Write the letters: ....

6 Which circuits contain a lamp with the same voltage across the lamp as that of the cell.

Write the letters: ....

> Acknowledgements

The authors and publishers acknowledge the following sources of copyright material and are grateful for the permissions granted. While every effort has been made, it has not always been possible to identify the sources of all the material used, or to trace all copyright holders. If any omissions are brought to our notice, we will be happy to include the appropriate acknowledgements on reprinting.

Thanks to the following for permission to reproduce images:

Cover Stephan Geist/EyeEm/GI; Inside **Unit 3** Bosca78/GI; Mphillips007/GI; **Unit 4** Jurgen&Christine Sohns/GI; **Unit 6** Peter Dazeley/GI; Pat Gaines/GI; **Unit 9** Jack Wild/GI

Key: GI= Getty Images